INFORMATION TECHNOLOGY IN 21ST CENTURY

INFORMATION TECHNOLOGY IN 21ST CENTURY

(In 9 Volumes)

WEB MARKETING

(Volume 8)

PROF. RAMESH CHANDRA

Vice-Chancellor, Bundelkhand University, Jhansi (U.P.)

Publication

KALPAZ PUBLICATIONS

DELHI–110052

INFORMATION TECHNOLOGY IN 21ST CENTURY
Web Marketing
(Information Technolgy)

Rs. 8000 (Set)
Rs. 900 (each volume)

ISBN: 81-7835-158-7 (Set)
ISBN: 81-7835-166-8 (Vol. 8)

Published in 2003 in India by
Kalpaz Publications
C-30, Satyawati Nagar
Delhi-110052
E-mail: kalpaz@hotmail.com

Laser Typesetting at: A.S. Printers
Printed at: Chawla Offset Printers, Delhi

Preface

The internet has taken its place beside the telephone and television as an important part of people's lives. Consumers around the world are increasingly turning to the internet to shop, bank and invest online. Because the World Wide Web is, as its name implies, worldwide, businesses that sell online can potentially reach billions of customers in every country of the world. Even small 'mom-n-pop' companies with websites are attracting a client base never before possible.

Business use of the worldwide network mostly involves information gathering with relatively few organisations actually purchasing products or services over the internet. Yet the internet is already proving its cost-effectiveness in purchasing and supply management, according to trade sources as diverse as leading business newspapers, specialised purchasing and supply management magazines, and reports from international organisations. Purchasing-related sites are on the rise, such as ones allowing businesses to track costs of raw materials and ones with online procurement requests.

As telecommunication infrastructure improves, and people become more comfortable with using the internet, organisations are starting to use a variety of tools to track purchases, manage stock levels, streamline ordering and payment processes. One can negotiate better prices for the products purchase by using the internet to monitor the material arid labour costs of your suppliers. If the product material contains a high percentage of commodities, one can monitor current market prices and trends in public online databases, and use this information when negotiating with suppliers.

The internet allows the customer in some cases to directly access manufacturers, and save money by avoiding costs of intermediaries. The internet reduces costs involved in order processing and invoice processing. It also lowers costs by reducing the number of dedicated telephone lines for fax machines normally required to move data. Strengthen relationships with suppliers that are linked with you electronically. One of the greatest benefits organisations can achieve by electronic linking with suppliers is substantial savings in inventory. Better communication links will decrease supply risks and shorten lead times, enabling you to adapt stock levels to the variations in demand more rapidly.

This book elaboratively describes new business operations and market opportunities the web provides. It will be highly beneficial to students, policy-makers, managers and marketing executives in the field of e-business.

Editor

Contents

1

Web Marketing

The last few decadses saw a host of emerging technologies emerge in a fragmented form. The mobile phone, the laptop computer, cable television, the fax and electronic mail systems seem certain to come together into flexible, quick and easy-to-use communication and information systems. The new information environment emphasises the needs to be met rather than the means used to satisfy them. Emphasis will be placed on needs, such as leisure or information, rather than specific and potentially outdated means of meeting them.

The new information technologies enhance the scope for novel combinations while increasing the competitive pressures on providers. They will create new options for provision and call for new patterns of behaviour such as: high availability, high customer specificity, recurrent adaptation, interaction and relationship marketing. The high availability of home and personal computers allied to the increasing penetration of television-based information services dramatically reduces the cost of information search.

Systems are transforming the current cumbersome access procedures while expanding the capacity for downloading material for reference and analysis. The internet originated to establish a public network to US defence interests, was gradually taken over by academic and specialist interests. Only recently have the commercial opportunities been recognised and exploited through speciality stores like the on-line bookstore Amazon and general stores like Wal-Mart in the USA. Amazon, the online bookstore, highlights the web's potential. It has no premises, originally operating out of the front room of its founder. It has access to over 2.3 million titles, and ships books around the world. It provides background and information that is impossible to deliver by conventional means. This background support includes expert reviews and even author comments. It is very difficult to predict the direction that computational technology will take over the next decade.

The newer, lower-price, easier-to-use systems provided an opportunity during the late 1980s to introduce a range of innovations especially suited to the trading practices and traditions of the retail and distributive sector. These include EFTS (electronic point of sale systems) and EFTS (electronic funds transfer systems). In particular they provide opportunities for decentralisation. They provides scope for storage, assembly and analysis of the vast number of transactions whose volume defeated earlier attempts to gather and use it effectively. There is increasing interest in the integration of retailing with the new technologies in a more active way. Many experiments have been tried: several have failed. Tesco's 'armchair shopping', i.e. where the items for sale are listed on the TV screen, made little headway in the face of customer resistance.

However, it is at the 'point of sale' that most immediate changes have taken place.

The introduction of electronic point of sale systems (EPOS) and associated bar coding systems gives firms the opportunity to store and retrieve accurate up-to-the minute information, print detailed till receipts, measure performance, improve cash control and price goods more accurately. Such improvements in the management functions have direct impacts on the marketing policies of the retailer and distributors and their relationships with manufacturers.

Traditional problems such as 'out of stock' difficulties should be drastically reduced, while the ability of the trader to monitor the performance of products will pose major challenges to the producers. Traders and suppliers use the new technology in, merchandising and promotion to improve layouts, quickly introduce special promotions, especially those based on price, and provide accurate information and promotional material for customers, perhaps using interactive video and computer graphics. The increased access to data provided by the new information technologies imposes extra responsibilities on management to use it effectively. This requires the construction of carefully planned and well-organised marketing information systems.

The MIS is the organised arrangement of people, machines and procedures set up to ensure that all relevant and usable information required by marketing management reaches them at a time and in a form to help them with effective decision-making. The marketing information systems are organised to ensure the most effective use of marketing, intelligence. This normally calls for planning, research, experimentation and introduction to ensure that the objectives of the MIS are achieved. Establishing these goals for the system is the first step. These aims should be as clearly defined and as fully understood as possible.

Specific responsibility for managing and monitoring the system is allocated to ensure continuing system efficiency as needs change and the range and variety of data develop. The system will only work if it is operated effectively. This calls for the integration of people, machines and procedures. People are frequently the primary sources of information as well as responsible for its efficient allocation and distribution. Machines are the tools of the system. It is a common fallacy that equipment can solve the problems in this area. It is generally more accurate to say that machines can only make good solutions work better. The marketing information systems helps to assist with effective decision-making. Some Management Information Systems (MIS), as well as much of the literature on MIS, are based on a significant misconception.

The assumption is made that the computer systems will benefit the management of the enterprise by providing more historical or projected data, of greater accuracy, in a more timely fashion, directly to the line manager for use in managing but very few line managers want more data than they now get whether historical or projected. Design of effective marketing information systems calls for the integration of the sources with needs. Piercy highlighted the degree to which conventional institutional barriers are eroded by modern information technologies. The integration of data from 'scanning', cable TV and Viewdata sources, besides more conventional means of gathering data, provides opportunities for manufacturers and retailers to cooperate to improve customer services. At the same time, new avenues for competition will emerge as firms realise that whoever controls the information system controls the market. Internet business strategy has nothing to do with hardware or software that comprise a system of networked computers; the emphasis is on core business concepts like the creation of a niche market, customer satisfaction, and so on. In other words, the stress is on human factors like creativity, determination, and vision.

The internet is only a business tool. Business use of the worldwide network mostly involves information gathering with relatively few organisations actually purchasing products or services over the internet. Yet the internet is already proving its cost-effectiveness in purchasing and supply management, according to trade sources as diverse as leading business newspapers, specialised purchasing and supply management magasines, and reports from international organisations. Purchasing-related sites are on the rise, such as ones allowing businesses to track costs of raw materials and ones with online procurement requests.

As telecommunications infrastructure improves, and people become more comfortable with using the internet, organisations are starting to use a variety of tools to track purchases, manage stock levels, streamline ordering and payment processes. One can negotiate better prices for the products purchase by using the internet to monitor the material arid labour costs of your suppliers. If the product material contains a high percentage of commodities, one can monitor current market prices and trends in public online databases, and use this information when negotiating with suppliers. Sources like Reuters commodities provide with both current and historical data on commodity futures and options prices, which can help you to hedge against future price rises. The internet can also help to analyse the labour costs involved in your purchased product Even without analysing the detailed material or labour costs of your supplies, you can use the internet as a benchmark for comparison with current prices paid, or for negotiating anticipated price rises. Try to access a server specialised in the market from which you are buying. You can often gather commercial information on your supply market, and also request suppliers connected to this site to quote you a price according to your specifications.

The internet allows you in some cases to directly access manufacturers, and save money by avoiding costs of intermediaries. The internet-when coupled with web-based EDI systems that incorporate a purchase order facility-reduces costs involved in order processing and invoice processing. It also lowers costs by reducing the number of dedicated telephone lines for fax machines normally required to move data. Strengthen relationships with suppliers that are linked with you electronically. One of the greatest benefits organisations can achieve by electronic linking with suppliers is substantial savings in inventory. Better communication links will decrease supply risks and shorten lead times, enabling you to adapt stock levels to the variations in demand more rapidly. Businesses are responding to a growing use of the internet by government: to disseminate procurement opportunities and receive quotations from interested providers.

International organisations are also using the internet for purchasing activities. Other concrete advantages of using internet-based tools include elimination errors due to rewriting or re-keying data, and speeding or re-keying data, and speeding up the payment process by processing invoices electronically. Companies that believe they do not have the time or money to invest in the internet for purchasing should consider how quickly the investment will be offset by reduced telecommunications costs. E-mail can be used with existing suppliers for most forms of communications including sending engineering specifications, negotiating, drafting contracts, and exchanging information at the price of a local phone call.

The internet and web-based EDI continuously improve information access and simplify the processes of ordering and payment. While they do not replace important routine purchasing activities such as supplier evaluations, visits or meetings, they offer an important opportunity to develop and manage day-to-day relations with suppliers that can lead to increased effectiveness and reduced costs in your purchasing operations. Although the gathering and analysis of data continues to be a central preoccupation of those involved in marketing, attention over the last few years has swung increasingly towards the issue of organisation and application of information. The net has the potential to transform the nature of trading relations by transferring real power to users and customers. The transfer of ideas, concepts and technologies on the internet exploits the interactive power of new communication and information technologies.

Internet provides its users the ability to migrate from one website to another almost without realising the complexity of the software tools that make this possible. One lesson from this is that a business seeking to provide value-added services should examine its ability to forge links with other complementary internet sites. Today, security of electronic transactions is of extremely high value to the customer. Because of the fear of subversive threats on the internet, such as traffic analysis, message deletion, message modification, spoofing, and password sniffing, electronic shoppers tend to do more looking/ surfing than actual buying. There is enough evidence to suggest that the educational element of an internet site is a key element of its success. Several organisations in a similar business come together to launch such sites to educate the public at large and, in turn, hope to build a clientele for their products/services that are founded on such good principles. The ability to individualise your internet presence for your customers, business partners, vendors, and even employees will go a long way in making you a successful company. The ability to move beyond meeting customer needs to actually anticipating those needs is the hallmark of a company striving to meet the challenges of a competitive market.

The internet makes proactivity easier. For example, in some advanced countries, supermarkets have software that can be used to discern the purchase patterns of frequent customers. This can then be used to provide information to those who wish to buy gifts for their friends or to come up with attractive discount schemes. The net allows a customer to collect and assess large quantities of information about specific products and services allowing a degree of comparison shopping previously unknown. People look upon the internet also a social medium for interaction.

Successful companies look at the internet as an opportunity to redefine the rules of business and the roles they play in providing new and better solutions.

After having decided to make the internet part of your business, it is important to understand your new operating environment. You need to develop new business models and assumptions, comparing and contrasting the old with the new, to determine the foundation on which your business is and will be based.

The most successful internet strategy offers more complete, convenient, and timely solutions for the customer than that available today. To envision new customer solutions, develop scenarios of your typical customers in their daily practices, incorporating your products or services into the picture. For this, the internet's ability to monitor the habits of consumers can be used to facilitate a better understanding of customer needs, values, and expectations. Internet technology can solve certain problems, and at times, can create opportunities. For example, the internet facilitates communication with suppliers, but it also creates new opportunities by offering more personalised and complete solutions to a global audience. It is important to recognise the difference between these two concepts, because you need to experiment with solutions to optimise and reengineer your business, as well as with new solutions that customers will value.

The internet customer does not reward the second to the market. The momentum generated by the first-to-market company can be a tremendous competitive obstacle for other companies. To design a phasing strategy, you need to outline business, marketing, and system objectives for each phase with the key business strategy steps. As web-based training advances, many non-proprietary causes will migrate to extranets so that customers and suppliers can access them. Because extranets are secure, companies will also find them valuable for collaborative research and product development. Extranet is a semi-private network, located outside the corporate firewall, which provides select internal information to business partners such as clients/ customers and suppliers as well as to remote employees. Thus, an extranet can be defined as a collaborative network that uses the internet technology to link businesses with their suppliers, customers, or other business partners that share common goals. An extranet can be viewed as part of a company's intranet that is made accessible to other companies. Extranets can be broadly classified as intronets and supranets. Intronet is an extranet where external trading partners have controlled access through the initiator's firewall to the intranet. Intronet is usually an inter-organisational decision-support system, where an external trading partner uses a standard web browser to enter into and retrieve any desired information from the client application. If an initiator company is able to provide unique, up-to-date, and valuable information, it gains competitive advantage through extranet. Companies should use a three-stage extranet strategy development process. They should first identify the technology constraints, which limit possible solutions, and only then turn to specific technology needs.

The best way of coping with the peculiarities of extranets is to identify a type or a model that best meets your objectives and the needs of your business partners. A model represents a typical combination of security and development choices aimed at specific business objectives and partners. The most complex extranets companies are building today follow the secured intranet access model. This is an extranet which allows business partners or raving employees direct access to the company's intranet via the internet or a dial-up infrastructure or a private IP network. The drawback of this model is that a higher cost is involved which negates much of the return on investment. The E-commerce extranet uses the same sort of security and network architecture as a business-to-business E-commerce site, but often is developed specifically for business-to-business transactions. It uses the secure sockets layer (SSL) protocol for encrypting and decrypting communication between the server and the client, session-by-session.

Extranets can be made more secure through demilitarised zones (DMZ), object request brokers (ORB), and virtual private networks (VPN). A DMZ can be made quite secure by setting up two firewalls: one that serves as the gateway from the DMZ to your corporate intranet, and another outside the firewall that lets partners into the DMZ servers from the external network. The DMZ approach uses a set of servers that are specifically designed as extranet servers. These may be web servers that have access permission for specified resources that are deemed appropriate for extranet partners. These servers should have extensive tracking and security-monitoring capabilities so that they function as a strong line of defence against intruders intent on breaching an intranet. When the extranet resources to be shared need to be maintained on more sensitive internal systems, an ORB is required that sits outside an inner firewall, and accepts and handles requests for resources. One firewall restricts access to proprietary resources while another allows limited but open access to resources. VPNs connect remote computers to a company's central network creating, in effect, a wide area network using the internet or a private network as the conduit.

Corporate intranet users are connected via Sprints IP service to corporate human resource applications, including payroll, benefits, and training. Through the extended intranet, more than 100,000 employees and 8,000 managers worldwide can go online to change direct deposit accounts and dependencies to health coverage, adjust their tax-filing codes, and perform other human resource functions. An extranet is available to distributors and dealers. It allows online access to more than 20,000 digitised image of current and former company products, such as tractors and lawn mowers. It includes search and retrieval facilities for images which are used heavily in company sales and marketing literature. The extranet also features traditional intranet elements, such as localised weather reports from the weather channel, stock ticker, daily company news reports, and a newsletter that covers the company's NASCAR racing team. The company offers field agents laptops and secure access to a data VPN, with access to centralised applications for contact management, customer need analysis, general account information, and sales illustrations.

Digital media professionals can use extranets to exchange files and access production service bureaus and printers online, while manufacturing and transportation industries can use it to interface with customers and suppliers. The automobile industry can exploit this technology to exchange CAD files and manage the inventory to save large amounts of money.

Internet marketing allows firms to develop new products and services and new market opportunities. By re-engineering business operations and service delivery, it brings added value and alters economies of scale. It can free work functions from location and time constraints, and by reorganising management structures, lead to flatter, leaner organisations.

The scope for low cost customisation is greatly increased, thereby opening opportunities for niche markets. Far more than being just a new channel for buying and selling, at its most extreme e-business involves major change in the enterprise's processes and culture. Indeed, to the extent that it involves wide-ranging change in business organisation and processes and potentially affects all companies, e-business is the ultimate innovation process. However, despite the acres of coverage devoted to e-business in the media it is seldom considered from an innovation standpoint. Management commentators tend to approach e-business from the perspective of corporate strategy, organisational theory or information systems.

Within the innovation literature, e-commerce is seen as one facet of wider socio-economic change, within framework referred to variously as the knowledge economy, the information society or the digital economy. The Small and Medium-sized Enterprises (SMEs) focus is pertinent because these firms are proving much more reluctant than large companies in adopting we marketing strategies. Encouraging and stimulating take-up of e-commerce in SMEs is emerging as a key public policy issue. SMEs are not a heterogeneous group.

There is increasing evidence of small businesses using e-commerce within business partnerships or associations. An increasing range of business functions are also being outsourced, from professional areas such as accountancy and law to IT services. And using internet applications, SMEs are banding together to build virtual organisations which appear to the customer to be a single business. All of these fall outside of the narrow B to C and 13 to B definitions commonly used in the literature. In the longer term, the most useful distinction is likely to be between customer-facing and supplier-facing e-commerce, where a customer may be a business customer or consumer. As a low cost communications medium, the internet gives small companies global reach. By effectively removing constraints of time and location, the net allows SMEs to access global markets much earlier in their lifecycles. It also allows them to develop closer and deeper links with their customers, providing greater security and opportunities for growth.

Governments are showing considerable interest in the SME sector and have put in place a whole variety of programmes aimed at addressing barriers. These focus on information provision, demonstration programmes, technical assistance and development of e-commerce platforms. Examples include paper and on-line information sources, demonstration centres, business simulations, and best practice case studies. The UK's Information Society Initiative and the US Small Business Agency provide links to manufacturers and suppliers of equipment, software and advice. France and Finland have funds to encourage internet use in SMEs. However, current policies are rather ad hoc. While governments are convinced that e-commerce can bring benefits for SMEs, their policy responses are highly pragmatic. A distinction need to be made between making businesses aware and actively encouraging implementation. Implementation environment in SMEs differs substantially from that of larger businesses. Firms are often young, less structured and less formal, with few fixed procedures or working practices. This lack of codification, together with limitations in IT capabilities, means SMEs usually have a less precise picture of their business processes or flows of business-related information.

Market characteristics are also a significant factor. With the exception of local retailing and services, SMEs' output is generally of low volume and high value, even to the extent of full customisation for each product or service. Moreover, firms may receive more than 80 per cent of their business from less than 20 per cent of their customers. Purchasing processes in such situations are sensitive and highly personalised. As part of a supply chain, SMEs may have to interface frequently with other suppliers and the ultimate customer, which also imposes constraints. Many of the e-commerce strategies used in large companies or in the retail sector are based on low value/high volume trading and so are not transferable, directly.

For traditional SMEs, this can lead to a vicious circle: in the absence of successful peer models firms remain unconvinced of the benefits of e-commerce, but without conviction new models do not arise. The financial restrictions on most SMEs reinforce this, so that where solutions are implemented it is on the basis of cost rather than strategic objective. In a study of around 200 SMEs in Manchester, Elsammani and Scown found that while SMEs perceived the importance of a web presence as being primarily for online sales, only 36 per cent had implemented such facilities in their sites. This and other studies suggest the web is still used mainly as a promotional medium. The type and size of web presence is also influenced by where the website is developed. As general awareness of e-commerce amongst the SME community rises, the emphasis in government programmes is shifting to implementation.

In a web-marketing environment, firms competitiveness depends not only on efficient internal organisation and optimal use of IT, but also on the depth, breadth and dynamism of their business partners. Faced with conflicting business drivers, companies are relying increasingly on networks of partners in order to create value. Thus, traditional value chains are giving way to virtual value nets involving complex relationships between suppliers, customers and intermediaries. Value networks represent a highly dynamic environment where competitive advantage accrues to the most mobile and responsive firms. With e-business, change processes reach beyond the firm and into the relationships and information flows between suppliers, customers and partners. In this networked view of the economy, competitiveness depends not only on the internal reorganisation of firms but also on the successful reorganisation of markets and the creation of new business models. Thus, e-business innovation is inherently systemic. As such, it involves interaction between many different economic actors. Although large firms have been the first movers, to the extent that most regional economies are dominated by small firms and public authorities, it is primarily through these actors that the effects of e-commerce will be felt at regional level.

Public authorities are especially important actors within this system, since they have a dual role both as facilitators/regulators and as actors within e-commerce makers in their own right. Moreover, the local and regional dimension is becoming increasingly important. Many SMEs are not and never will be global suppliers. For them the most significant feature of e-commerce is not its global reach but the ability to connect into local markets and supply chains.

In the e-commerce environment networks assume even greater significance. This is partly because of the scale and reach of the change and partly because the internet itself facilitates new forms of networking interaction. As a result, we are seeing the emergence both of new networked-based business models and non-commercial virtual communities. New business models include aggregators, auctions and exchanges—each of which attacks different market inefficiencies. Aggregators put buyers in touch with sellers by pooling content within a searchable, business-oriented trading environment. Auctions create markets and reduce sellers' losses. Buyers pit against each other to purchase sellers' surpluses without accruing real-world search or travel costs. Klang suggests a matrix approach, classifying virtual communities according to their legal basis and motivation. This gives rise to categories such as the Club, the Shop and the Bazaar Klang, further argues that, virtual communities are dynamic and that as they evolve changes in format and emphasis can put such communities under strain. As the face of work and leisure change, online communities are likely to become increasingly important determinants of the behaviour of individuals and firms. Not all e-commerce networks are virtual, however. Indeed, rather than decreasing real-world interaction, the pace of the net seems to reinforce the role of traditional business networks in being able to innovate successfully.

Virtually every business, from the smallest SME to the largest multinational will be affected. Each has to assess how the new networked approach to business will affect them and respond accordingly. Faced with a challenge of this magnitude existing innovation structures appear to be totally inadequate. And in any case, the majority of firms have limited interaction with the formal innovation infrastructure. This suggests we have to look to alternative ways to support e-business innovation in SMEs. For smaller companies, in particular, support agencies need to cater for a continuum of needs rather than a discrete package. This requires e-business support policies to focus on the whole growth process, with the emphasis on business objectives rather than technology. Mentoring support can help SMEs articulate and develop their business and IT strategies. Furthermore, customised support packages must recognise the increasing maturity of client companies as they become familiar with e-business models. Models of e-business as an innovation system need to characterise other actors in a similar way and to analyse and explain interactions between them.

The SME/large company, SME/public authority and SME/intermediary interfaces appear to be particularly important. Currently, we have little information on supply chain pressures as a factor in e-commerce innovation. And of course such models also need to take account of 'environmental parameters', such as the role of regulation and access to infrastructure, both key areas in current e-commerce policies. Net start-ups for whom the internet is their sole marketplace, new business models which transcend traditional market structures; virtual communities which have both economic and social features. As yet we know very little about the innovation behaviour of these entities. The innovation perspective also underlines the importance of the regional dimension in e-commerce policies. The key policy challenge is to embed e-business practices in SMEs and public authorities, both of which are rather conservative in innovation terms. SMEs are just one part of an e-commerce innovation system. Attempts to explain and influence their behaviour must take account of this wider environment.

Berranger and Tucker describe the introduction of e-commerce practices to creative businesses in Manchester. The project used well-established informal communication networks together with change agents carefully chosen for their understanding of the particular business sector. Information and training were tailored to the requirements of each SME so that they could appreciate how e-commerce could be of direct benefit to their individual business. The fact that change agents were well informed and had located close to the participants was important in overcoming the barriers to trust. And the physical proximity of the change agents facilitated training that was closely matched to immediate business needs. In a pilot project run by Cardiff University selected SMEs used a test platform of selected technologies and applications to experience the benefits of electronic trading at first hand. All of the SMEs realised real business benefits. These ranged from the tangible, to quasi-tangible, to the intangible. Based on these positive experiences, companies were keen to learn more about how the technologies and applications could be used. While these approaches go some way to explaining SMEs' experiences of e-commerce, there is a need for a much deeper understanding of implementation and diffusion.

Guidelines for Internet Marketing

Some basic aspects which will be beneficial to all who are in the field of internet marketing are given below:

— Whether you have recently been given responsibility for getting your business on the Web or to handle a pre-existing Web site, there are some general truths (at least in this consultant's eyes) that you should strongly consider.

— Do not consider the Internet simply as a place to put your brochures in electronic form. Do not make the mistake of treating the Internet as if it is simply an advertising medium. The Web has more in common with the telephone than print. It is different from traditional media in many respects. Even Internet advertising requires a different approach than off-line advertising. Exploit the Web's unique qualities to provide a richer experience for customers and prospects.

— Find out what your competitors are doing on the Web. Spend a few days checking out how your competitors are using the Web. Analyze each site. How does the site help tell the world about that company's products or services; is it easy to use; is it enjoyable to use; does it add value to the company's customer service; is it integrated with the company's other marketing efforts.

— Create an Internet business plan and live it. Before starting your company's Web site project, determine measurable goals and objectives for your company's site, establish milestones. Make them both qualitative and quantitative. This may sound obvious, but planning is one of the most neglected areas of corporate Web site management. Your Internet business strategy should be an extension of your company's existing business strategy and well-integrated with everything your company does off-line.

— Don't be inconsistent with your off-line brand. Make sure your Web site experience is consistent with your brand image. For instance, is your brand known for superior engineering and being easy-to-use? Make sure your Web site experience is consistent. A recent study found that corporate Web site email responses are highly informal and unbranded.

— Email marketing works, but be careful. Email marketing is one of the most effective ways to stay in touch with customers and prospects online. It can also be effective as a direct-marketing device. My advice to B2B marketers, in most cases, do not rent email lists, build your own. Do not rent out your list. Never spam, under any circumstances. Let email subscribers know in advance how often you will send messages and what type of content they can expect. Make messages as targeted as possible; relevancy keeps people listening.

— Be sure your Web site is integrated with your company's other marketing activities. Don't make the mistake some traditional companies do and create an Internet effort that is disconnected with your company's off-line efforts. Your Web site should be connected with your company's off-line efforts. This means more than throwing the company Web address in your ads.

— Segment and target. Even without sophisticated personalization technology, the Web allows you to easily target your messages, making them more relevant to users. Find out who they are in the least intrusive way possible and then talk to them more personally.

— Use your company's Web site to enhance customer service — especially for prospects who may be researching. The Internet allows your company to stay in touch with its customers and provide them with answers to questions they are likely to ask. Make sure your site makes it easy for your customers to find what they want and communicate with your company. A good corporate Web site helps current customers and develops new customers too. Consider real-time online help systems.

— Make your site an information resource for its target markets. Becoming a trusted resource of high quality information for your customers is of tremendous value to your business, in addition, it can help win your company free press and word-of-mouth/mouse.

— Do user testing. If you have the budget, do usability testing prior to launching your Web site. Bring in an expert usability group — don't merely rely on the company that developed your site, bring in another, unrelated usability testing firm. If you cannot afford to do formal testing with a usability group, I would recommend you bring in a usability expert and afterwards, test with several of your customers.

— Care about privacy. Even though most users don't bother to read privacy policies, studies show they do care. My guess is that this will only increase over time. Make sure you have a good privacy policy and a privacy statement on your site that is easy to find and customer friendly. Build your privacy policy around your customers' concerns. When it comes to email, never send out unsolicited email (spam), it not only damages your reputation and could get you into hot water, it also has extremely low response rates.

— Be ready for inquiries. Most corporate Web sites are horrible about responding to email inquiries, don't let yours be one. Also, be ready for international business inquiries, even if it means telling visitors you don't handle out of country orders.

— Outsource areas your company does not have expertise. If you plan on getting real value out of your Web site, outsourcing its development to the right firm is critical. I would recommend that you find a firm with marketing experience, not just designers and computer programmers. Remember that a designer's expertise is in design, a programmer's expertise is in programming and an Internet marketer's expertise is in Internet marketing.

— Keeping up with the rapid changes of Internet marketing is a full time job. Find an expert and use him or her. Concentrate your efforts on running your business or handling your professional responsibilities.

— Promote Your Web site. There is a popular misconception that Web sites do not need to be promoted. Consider that some of the Web's biggest successes spend about 75% of their advertising budgets on non-Internet media. Having a Web site is like having a toll-free number that's not listed in every phone book...you need to work hard to drive visitors to your Web site. As with any other media, it costs money to make it a success. Plaster your Web site address (URL) everywhere you can — at trade show appearances, on business cards, stationary, in ads and everywhere else you can think of.

— Use Internet advertising where it makes sense. Internet advertising has been pushed as a direct-response device, but the B2B process is far more complex and longer than with B2C. Where a B2C ad may attempt to get a consumer to make a purchase, this is not realistic for high-ticket B2B items. Instead, B2B marketers should consider using Internet advertising to reach targets that regularly use the Internet at the places they often go with ads that feature things like white papers, research, Web seminars and other information that is likely to be of strong interest to prospects.

— Give it away free. For B2B marketers, the Internet provides a great opportunity to provide your target markets with high quality intellectual capital that can help position your company as a thought leader in the minds of your target markets.

— Continuously analyze your Web traffic and other e-metrics to learn and improve. Find out how people are getting to your site and what they're doing once they get there. Any good Web site statistics software package will tell you how many people are going to your site, what pages they're viewing, what search engines they're coming from and more. If you're using a Web development firm, make sure that they review this with you on no less than a quarterly basis. Find out what's working and what's not. Redesign your site to make it more effective for your users and for reaching your desired objectives (e.g., get leads, sales, etc.). Integrate your on-line and off-line information to provide a more complete picture of customers and prospects.

2

Marketing Paradigms for E-Commerce

The rapid adoption of the Internet as a commercial medium has caused firms to experiment with innovative ways of marketing to consumers in computer-mediated environments. These developments on the Internet are expanding beyond the utilization of the Internet as a communication medium to an important view of the Internet as a new market.

The most exciting commercial developments are occurring on that portion of the Internet known as the World Wide Web (WWW). The WWW is a distributed hypermedia environment within the Internet which was originally developed by the European Particle Physics Laboratory (CERN).

Global hypermedia allows multimedia information to be located on a network of servers around the world which are interconnected, allowing one to travel through the information by clicking on hyperlinks. Any hyperlink (text, icon or image in a document) can point to any document anywhere on the Internet. The user-friendly consumer-oriented homepages of the WWW utilize the system of hyperlinks to simplify the task of navigating among the offerings on the Internet.

The present popularity of the WWW as a commercial medium is due to its ability to facilitate global sharing of information and resources, and its potential to provide an efficient channel for advertising, marketing, and even direct distribution of certain goods and information services.

Commercialisation of Web

Anecdotal evidence suggests that Web-based commercial efforts are more efficient and possibly even more effective than efforts mounted in traditional channels. Initial conjectures on efficiencies generated by online commercial efforts suggests that marketing on the Web results in "10 times as many units [sold] with 1/10 the advertising budget". It is about one-fourth less costly to perform direct marketing through the Net than through conventional channels. This fact becomes especially critical in the face of shrinking technology and product life cycles and increasing technological complexity. Consider the example of SunSolve Online , which has saved Sun Microsystems over $4 million in FAQs alone since they "reengineered information processes around the WWW".

Firms use various media to communicate with their current and potential customers. Marketing communications perform three functions: to inform, to remind, and to persuade. In this passive model, firms provide content through a medium to a mass market of consumers. The first two functions of marketing communications may be performed by a traditional communication model. However, the persuasion function necessary for differentiating a product or brand is limited by the unidirectionality of traditional mass media.

The Internet, a revolution in distributed computing and interactive multimedia many-to-many communication, is dramatically altering this traditional view of communication media. The new many-to-many marketing communications model defining the Web offers a radical departure from traditional marketing environments.

The Internet offers an alternative to mass media communication. Some applications on the Internet represent "narrowcasting" to the extreme, with content created by consumers and for consumers. As a marketing and advertising medium, the Web has the potential to change radically the way firms do business with their customers by blending together publishing, real-time communication broadcast and narrowcast. As an operational model of distributed computing, the "Net" supports:

— Discussion groups (e.g., USENET news, moderated and unmoderated mailing lists),

— Multi-player games and communications systems (e.g., MUDs, irc, chat, MUSEs),

— File transfer (ftp) and remote login (telnet),

— Electronic mail ("email"), and

— Global information access and retrieval systems (e.g., archie, veronica, gopher, and the World Wide Web).

From a business and marketing perspective, the most exciting developments are occurring on that portion of the Internet known as the World Wide Web. In this chapter, we present an initial attempt to organize the commercial activity on the Web thus far according to its business function. We identify two major categories of sites: "Destination Sites," and "Web Traffic Control Sites." Under destination sites, we identify Online Storefronts, Internet Presence Sites, and Content Sites. These comprise the ultimate "destinations" housing a firm's virtual counterpart. The purpose of the Web Traffic Control Sites is to direct consumers to these various Destination Sites. There are three major categories of Web Traffic Control: Malls, Incentive Sites, and Search Agents. We argue for considering our framework in the context of "integrated marketing," in which various communications vehicles are coordinated to create a single, strategically appropriate marketing effort to maximize customer response.

As a commercial medium, the Web offers a number of important benefits which can be examined at both the customer and firm levels. In this way, we can address both demand and supply issues. We discuss the buyer benefits first, followed by the firm benefits. Buyer benefits arise primarily from the structural characteristics of the medium and include availability of information, provision of search mechanisms, and online product trial, all of which can lead to reduced uncertainty in the purchase decision. Firm benefits arise from the potential of the Web as a distribution channel, a medium for marketing communications, and a market in and of itself. These efficiencies are associated with Web technology and the interactive nature of the medium.

One important consumer benefit associated with marketing on the Web is the access to greater amounts of dynamic information to support queries for consumer decision making. The Hermes survey of Web users found gathering purchase-related information was the most preferred Web activity. Further, the interactive nature of the Web and the hypertext environment allow for deep, nonlinear searches initiated and controlled by customers. Hence marketing communications on the Web are more consumer-driven than those provided by traditional media. In addition, recreational uses of the medium, manifested in the form of nondirected search behavior, can be an important benefit to consumers intrinsically motivated to use the medium.

The ability of the Web to amass, analyze, and control large quantities of specialized data can enable comparison shopping and speed the process of finding items. The Web facilitates trial and provides instant gratification; customers can test products online which may stimulate purchase. There is also the potential of wider availability of hard-to-find products and wider selection of items due to the width and efficiency of the channel.

In addition to the above, the advantages for industrial consumers are reduced costs to buyers from increased competition in procurement as more suppliers are able to compete in an electronically open marketplace. This increase in competition leads to better quality and variety of goods through expanded markets and the ability to produce customized goods.

Firm benefits arise partly from the use of the Web as a distribution channel. First, the Web potentially offers certain classes of providers participation in a market in which distribution costs or cost-of-sales shrink to zero. This is most likely for firms in publishing, information services or digital product categories. For example, digital products can be delivered immediately, hence such businesses may encounter massive disintermediation or even the eventual elimination of middleman. Moreover buyers and sellers can access and contact each other directly, potentially elmininating some of the marketing cost and constraints imposed by such interactions in the terrestrial world. This may also have the effect of shrinking the channel and making distribution much more efficient (mainly due to reduced overhead costs through such outcomes as uniformity, automation, and large-scale integration of management processes). Time to complete business transactions may be reduced as well, translating into additional efficiencies for the firm. However, such potential efficiencies must be tempered with market realities.

Second, business on the Web transfers more of the selling function to the customer, through online ordering and the use of fill-out forms, thus helping to bring transactions to a conclusion. This permits a third benefit in the form of capture of customer information.

The technology offers the firm the opportunity to gather market intelligence and monitor consumer choices through customers' revealed preferences in navigational and purchasing behavior in the Web. Note however that there are many social, legal and technological issues and drawbacks at the present level of technology which prevent firms from fully capitalizing on this benefit.

At the present time, most firms use the Web primarily to deliver information about the firm and its offerings and for both internal and external communication with other firms and consumers. The interactive nature of the medium offers another category of firm benefits since it is especially conducive to developing customer relationships. This potential for customer interaction, which is largely asynchronous under current implementations, facilitates relationship marketing and customer support to a greater degree than ever before possible with traditional media.

Web sites are available on demand to consumers 24 hours a day. The interactive nature of the medium can be used by marketers to hold the attention of the consumer by engaging the consumer in an asynchronous "dialogue" that occurs at both parties' convenience.

This capability of the medium offers unprecedented opportunities to tailor communications precisely to individual customers, allowing individual consumers to request as much information as desired. Further, it allows the marketer to obtain relevant information from customers for the purpose of serving them more effectively in the future.

The simplest implementations involve engaging customers through the use of email buttons located strategically on the site. More sophisticated implementations may involve fill-out forms and other incentives designed to engage customers in ongoing relationships with the firm.

The objective of such continuous relationship-building is dual-pronged: to give consumers information about the firm and its offerings and to receive information from consumers about their needs with respect to such offerings. Hence, effective customized advertising, promotion and customer service is the fifth benefit that the commercial Web offers to the firm.

Most importantly, the Web offers opportunity for competition on the "specialty" axis instead of the price axis. From a marketing perspective, it is rarely desirable to compete solely on the basis of price. Instead, marketers attempt to satisfy needs on the basis of benefits sought (TK), which means pricing is dependent upon value to the consumer, not costs. Such opportunity arises when the offering is differentiated by elements of the marketing mix other than price. This results in the delivery of value-laden benefits, for example, convenience through direct electrónic distribution of software, or enjoyment through a visually-appealing and unusual Web site.

As evidence that this is occurring, consumers indicated that price was the least important product attribute considered when making online purchases. The ability to compete on dimensions other than price will become especially critical in categories where brands are perceived as substitutes, since it allows for more opportunities to differentiate along other dimensions.

Operational benefits of Web use for industrial sellers are reduced errors, time, and overhead costs in information processing; reduced costs to suppliers by electronically accessing on-line databases of bid opportunities, online abilities to submit bids, and online review of awards. In addition, creation of new markets and segments, increased generation of sales leads, easier entry into new markets and faster time to market is facilitated. This is due to the ability to reach potential customers easily and cheaply and eliminate delays between the different steps of the business subprocesses.

The barriers to consumer and firm adoption impact critical mass. Accumulated industry experience and anecdotal evidence strongly support the contention that the primary barrier to consumer adoption of the Web as a commercial medium is ease of access. Convenience of access is at the core of the adoption of any technological application and determines its ultimate success. In the context of the Web, ease of access is a multidimensional construct and includes high speed access (the "bandwidth" problem), ease of finding a service provider, and the diffusion of the computer hardware/software/modem bundle into the home.

The secondary barriers are ease of use, price, and risk, including such factors as privacy and security. Ease of use includes issues such as the user-friendliness of the software, ease of software installation, and the like. The marketplace will weed out even technically feasible Web applications if they prove too complicated for the average consumer to use. Hence attempts to develop technology that is user- friendly are as important as the development of the technology itself.

There is a great deal of concern regarding the security of financial information transmitted over the Internet and its impact on consumer willingness to buy or sell products. This limitation is critical to mass adoption of the Web, especially since surveys of Web users indicate that vendor reliability and security of financial transactions are important to users. At this writing, such limitations impact consumer behavior on the Web: currently, the majority of consumers use the Web to browse or search much more than actually to purchase something.

The barriers to firm adoption arise from the Web measurement problem. Firms are unsure of the number of people on the Net and how many people use the Web and this uncertainty makes investment decisions difficult. In addition, there are no established criteria for judging the success of Web sites. Hence, researchers need to develop concepts to shape standards. Such standards are critical to demonstrate the viability of the Web as a commercial medium, and provide mechanisms for measuring investment opportunities and business success.

The commercial success of a firm's Web site depends in part on accurate information on market potential and consumer needs. The Web provides multiple ways to reach a diverse and exciting set of markets. Determining the appropriate set of target market segments and evaluating the penetration of Web access technology in each market is the first step in developing an integrated marketing strategy.

Because critical mass for interactive technologies is "all-or-none," the Web will not be successful as a commercial medium until it achieves critical mass. An important first step in any marketing program is therefore the determinat ion of how many people are on the Internet and what they are doing there. It is also necessary to define and estimate segments of Web behavior based on customer need.

The economics of the Web can then be examined for each specific case to determine if the return on investment meets financial targets. Some sites, e.g., Pathfinder , HotWired , and Internet Shopping Network are attempting to capture data to address the above objectives by providing the option for visitor "authentication."

In this process, visitors may register as subscribers in order to use the site fully. This enables the marketer to use demographic data and information on new and repeat visit patterns to strengthen its (and sponsors') marketing programs on the site. Ultimately, marketers may build detailed databases and tailor marketing programs specifically to individual visitors or groups of visitors.

Models of Web-Based Business

Consider the following. As of October 9, 1995, a significant number of the 80,000-plus Web servers on the Internet represent commercial sites. Nearly 14,000 firms were listed in Open Market's "Commercial Services on the Net" directory and in the Yahoo Business and Economic directory, there were 23,540 entries under "Companies," with an additional distribution of listings as follows:

Yahoo Heading	Number of Sites
Classifieds	262
Directories	178
E-Commerce	67
Marketing	46
Markets and Investments	308
Products and Services	4431

There is no doubt that a great deal of commercial activity exists on the Web and that this activity is increasing. However, the proliferation is confusing. What sorts of business models are being implemented? Are some better than others? Two questions are especially relevant:

1) Is anyone making any money? And
2) Where are the opportunities?

Profitability from commercial activity on the Web includes productivity savings, marketing and sales savings, and incremental or new revenue streams. Productivity savings arise from reduction in order and processing costs and more efficient inventory management. Increases in productivity on the "soft" side through more efficient personnel may also lead to productivity gains.

Savings may also be realized from efficiences in the marketing and selling functions. The Web shifts more of these functions to the customer; savings result through reduced brochure printing and distribution costs and reductions in order-taking as c ustomers use fill-out forms to prepare their own orders. As control is also effectively transferred to the customer, we speculate that customer satisfaction might actually be increased.

Finally, incremental or new revenue streams are available for firms participating in digital commerce, through, for example, online sales, advertising revenues, or information brokering. Incremental revenues may be achieved for those firms who use the Web to expand into new channels of distribution and new market segments. Corporate training, electronic distribution and maintenance provide additional revenue opportunities for appropriate firms. However, secure mechanisms for transactions are necessary to fully exploit the revenue-generating opportunities of the Web.

Although we can address the potential for profitability, the question of whether anyone is making money on the Web remains largely premature. However, a careful examination of where the opportunities are can be undertaken. Despite the current frenzy of activity, there is little information on the types of business models in use and whether some have the potential to be more effective than others. Strategic insight is therefore needed into how sites are differentiated, how they may be designed more effectively, and how to attract customers to sites.

Classification of Commercial Web Sites

In integrated marketing programs, marketing managers combine elements of various media in order to maximize the effectiveness of a communications program. Despite the intense interest in such coordinated efforts, there has yet to be widespread adoption and implementation of the concept. The concept of integrated marketing holds appeal and promise for business efforts on the World Wide Web, because the Web offers enormous potential for developing customer relationships and customizing the offering to individual customers.

In this section, we define six functional categories of Commercial Web Pages. Each can be considered as an element in an integrated marketing program in the context of digital commerce. Below we discuss each category in detail and suggest how the elements may combine structurally to form the components of an integrated marketing program. The examples presented below were selected to reflect the range of practice regarding commercial activity on the Web, not necessarily best business practice. The reader should also be aware that as the Web is rapidly evolving, some links may have changed or disappeared altogether.

— Online Storefront

— Internet Presence (Flat Ad, Image and Information)

— Content (Fee-Based, Sponsored, Searchable Database)

— Mall

— Incentive Site

— Search Agent

The six functional types provide the building blocks for a successese, put to different use. Commercial Web site design includes Online Storefront sites, Internet Presence sites and Content sites. The main challenges for marketers are to attract visitors to the site and generate significant repeat visits. Awareness leads to trial or the initial site visit so that the trial problem depends on "Web Traffic Control." However, sites will only be successful in the long run if they generate repeat traffic, which is far more difficult to achieve than trial. The repeat visit problem is partly a function of Web site design and depends to a large extent on customer need.

Online Storefront

These Web sites offer direct sales through an electronic channel via an electronic catalog or other, more innovative format. The number of products presently being sold on a single site ranges from one to many. Consumers order goods via fill-out form, 800 number, registration, or surface mail.

Online storefronts cover a wide variety of offerings; examples include Absolutely Fresh Flowers , Adventurous Travelers Bookstore , Alaska River Adventures , Ann Hemyng Candy , CDNow, Freeway Enterprises Person-to- Person Web Sites & Greeting Cards , HeadFirst, Internet Shopping Network , San Francisco Music Box Company, and Shrink- Link. . A recent innovator in this category is Security First Network Bank, FSB, the world's first Internet bank. This entry offers online consumers the ability to open accounts, pay bills, and manage their finances via the World Wide Web.

Opportunities abound for the Online Storefront model. It combines elements of direct marketing with in-store shopping and has the potential to be vastly more efficient than either. In this approach, there are tremendous opportunities for customization and relationship marketing. A much broader definition of product and service categories becomes possible in this environment. The ultimate development are those products that can exist or be consumed only on the Web.

However, the Online Storefront model poses a number of Challenges. Current access speeds can make online shopping frustrating and tedious. Additionally, the terrestrial approach to shopping necessarily sets the standards for online offerings. In many cases, the online versions pale in comparison to real-world experiences of flipping through glossy catalogues or shopping in department stores.

Because the technologies for secure transactions are not mature yet, security and privacy are major issues that have yet to be addressed satisfactorily in this medium. Finally, the consumer behavior issues are completely unknown. For example, we have little idea how to stimulate "trial" and "repeat," do not know yet what the most effective segmentation bases will be for online shopping and understand little about the impact of marketing tools like custom-designed incentives.

Internet Presence Sites

Internet presence sites provide a virtual "presence" for a firm and its offerings. They may also serve to signal to current and prospective customers and competitors that the firm is on the cutting edge, possibly driven by "mimetic isomorphism". We identify three types of Internet Presence sites: flat ad, image, and information.

Flat Ads are single page electronic flyers with no hypermedia links. They could just as easily appear in a newspaper or magazine, though a flat ad is decidedly less sophisticated than its print counterparts. We expect the evolution in this category to include hypermedia, particularly as Web browsers like Netscape integrate real-time audio and video. Weightlifting 101 and Xopix represent current examples of flat ads.

In Internet Presence Image sites, the consumer appeal is emotional rather than rational. Information about the product, if any, is provided in the context in which the product is consumed, or has meaning to the consumer. Such sites appear to be especially suited to products that have low hard-information content. Information sites provide detailed, rational information about the firm and/or its offerings.

Internet Presence Information sites can take on innovative and sophisticated forms (for example, Sun Microsystems), and are best suited to offerings with high degree of hard-information content. Decision aids (e.g. "Step Search,") can be used to facilitate navigation.

One objective of such sites is to build a relationship with the consumer even before the need to purchase the product or service arises. Examples include American Airlines , Andersen Consulting , Apple Computer , Burlington Coat Factory , Club Med , FedEx , Fidelity Investments , Forrester Research , HeadsTogether/ Bookworm , Lotus , MathSoft , Network Wizards , and Volvo .

Opportunities for Internet Presence sites include the ability to reach motivated customers with an information- or image-rich communications message. Because the entry barriers are so low, smaller firms can set up Internet Presence sites as well (or in some cases even better) than larger firms. We believe that Internet Presence sites represent the future of advertising and marketing communications on the Web. Challenges include the actual execution, that is, what is the best way to implement such a concept? Executional challenges are greater for image sites, but the rewards may be greater, as well, since image sites are possibly more likely to generate flow, the "glue" holding the user in a site. A final challenge is how managers can evaluate the effectiveness of such sites.

Content

In Fee-Based content sites, the provider supplies and/or pays for content which the consumer pays to access. Fee-based content sites are expected to proliferate as secure payment mechanisms are implemented. To date, however, the model has met with only limited success, perhaps because consumers may be unwilling to pay for content delivered in this manner.

A recent trend is toward information-brokering, as with Newshare, and usage-based pricing, as with NewsPage, where visitors are able to access news summaries at no charge, but incur a small fee for the full text of a story. Other examples include DowVision, QuoteCom, and Washington Weekly.

Sponsored content sites sell advertising space to reduce or eliminate the necessity of charging fees to visitors. Thus, as with magazines in the terrestrial world, advertising appears from a variety of sources and underwrites the editorial content. A recent trend is toward sponsored "entertainment" content (e.g., The World Wide Web Dating Game), and sponsored search agents. Typical current examples of sponsored content sites include HotWired , Mother Jones , PowerPC News , Triangle Online , and Washingtonian Online . Some sponsored content sites combine elements of the Internet Presence model and the Mall. Examples of such hybrids include GNN , MecklerWeb , and Pathfinder . Current advertising rate structures and information on sponsored content sites is available from Interactive Publishing Alert.

In the third type of content model, merchants or advertisers pay a provider for information placement in an organized listing in a Searchable Database. The unit of analysis is a person, service, or information source, all of the same type. This is the inverse of Fee-Based content model. Selected examples include Catalog Mart Home Page , Single-Search , and the Virtual Headbook .

Opportunities abound for content sites, as they closely parallel traditional media models. At the present time, there is generally no (sponsored content) or at most a small (fee-based) charge to consumers to consume the content. For some firms, e.g., Wired and Time/Warner, they offer a new channel for expansion.

Firms adopting this model have the opportunity to reach an advertiser-coveted audience. In addition, such sites may provide meaningful exposure that would otherwise be lost in the unstructured clutter that currently typifies the Web. Additionally, content sites can demonstrate innovation, are efficient compared to their terrestrial counterparts, and are, in theory, easy to implement. However, the challenges for content sites arise due to this perceived ease of implementation. The close parallels to traditional media represent significant execution hurdles for content sites. How best to measure and optimize consumer response to advertising in sponsored content sites is completely unknown.

Mall

The Mall site typically constitutes a collection of online storefronts, each of which may contain many different categories of goods for sale. The provider charges rent in exchange for the virtual real-estate and may offer a variety of services to the storefront. Some malls also accept advertising, as with, for example, the Internet Mall. Other examples include the Branch Mall , CyberMart, eMall , and Shopping 2000.

Incentive Site

The Incentive Site represents a unique form of advertising that attracts a potential customer to a site. The objective is to pull the user to the commercial site behind it, thus helping marketers generate traffic to their Web sites. The content may be transitory in nature and may appear to serve as a "public service announcement" or offer incentives. From the context of web traffic control, Incentive Sites serve the same function as Malls. Some efforts may be especially sophisticated, as in directory services like Open Market. Other examples include As the Web Turns , Cupid's Cove, and Lucky Leprechaun's Lane.

Search Agents

The purpose of Search Agent sites is to identify other Web sites through keyword search of a database that extends throughout the Web. Software agents are used to generate and/or assist the search through the database. A recent trend in such sites is the emergence of fee-based (e.g., InfoSeek) or advertiser-sponsored (e.g. Yahoo) search agents. Other examples are Lycos, Open Text, and Web Crawler, with additional contenders entering the market regularly. Newer search agents like BargainFinder incorporate increased assistance to the user in the search pro cess.

In terms of opportunities, there are a wide variety of novel ways of generating traffic to a Destination Web site. There is also the potential to model the diffusion of site visitors as a function of the location from which the consumer entered the site. Recently, search agent sites have shown potential as high-traffic vehicles for advertising sponsorship. Web traffic control sites face a number of challenges. The proliferation of commercial Web sites means that it is increasingly difficult to find anything on the Web, especially if one is not looking for it. Therefore, identifying pivotal cross-linking opportunities will be critical.

Marketing Paradigms

The World Wide Web is the first and current networked global implementation of a hypermedia computer mediated environment (CME). As such, it allows users of the medium to provide and interactively access hypermedia content, and to communicate with each other. These unique forms of interactivity, "machine-interaction" and "personinteraction," respectively, have contributed to the rapid diffusion of the Web as a commercial medium in the last several years.

The traditional marketing communications model for mass media holds that mass communication is a one-to-many process whereby a firm transmits content through a medium to a large group of consumers. The key feature underlying all models of mass media effects is that there is no interaction present between consumers and firms.

The new model underlying marketing communications in a hypermedia CME like the Web is a many-to-many mediated communications model in which consumers can interact with the medium, firms can provide content to the medium, and in the most radical departure from traditional marketing environments, consumers can provide commercially-oriented content to the medium.

In this mediated model, the primary relationships are not between sender and receiver, but rather with the CME with which they interact. In this new model, information or content is not merely transmitted from a sender to a receiver, but instead, mediated environments are created by participants and then experienced.

An important consideration in the structural analysis of the Web as a media and marketing environment is that it possesses unique characteristics which distinguish it in important ways from traditional commercial environments. First, as we argued above, the Web is a virtual hypermedia environment incorporating interactivity with both people and computers. Thus, the Web is not a simulation of a real-world environment, but an alternative to real world environments, where consumers may experience telepresence , the perception of being present in the mediated, rather than real-world, environment.

Second, within the virtual environment, both experiential (e.g. "netsurfing") and goal-directed (e.g. "online shopping") behaviors compete for consumers' attention. Third, consumer capability in the virtual environment, as well as challenges posed by the environment, introduce a competency issue which does not exist so fundamentally in the physical world. This competency issue involves flow, which is the "process of optimal experience" achieved when a motivated consumer perceives a balance between their skills and the challenges of their interaction with the CME. Flow is a central construct when considering consumer navigation on commercial Web sites.

Because the World Wide Web presents a fundamentally different environment for marketing activities than traditional media, conventional marketing activities are being transformed, as they are often difficult to implement in their present form. This means that in many cases, these marketing activities have to be reconstructed in forms more appropriate for the new medium.

This process of transformation and reconstruction of marketing and communication activities in information-intensive environments has been noted by numerous researchers. In order to maintain a virtual community on the Internet, Reid, for example, has argued that users have had to deconstruct and reconstruct the nonverbal communication that exists in interpersonal communication by typing their feelings out *and* constructing a notational system to convey emotion. In addition, the online medium has the potential to transform the individual's identity, resulting in a relative anonymity of users in these environments. In a marketing context, this hinders personal selling at the same time that it encourages negative word fouth activity.

Most important from a marketing perspective, however, is the manner in which the Web transforms the marketing function. For example, the many to many communication model turns traditional principles of mass media advertising inside out, rendering application of advertising approaches which assume a passive, captive consumer difficult, if not impossible. Thus, marketers must reconstruct advertising models for the interactive, many to many medium underlying the Web in which consumers actively choose whether or not to approach firms through their Web sites, and exercise unprecedented control over the management of the content they interact with. Informational and image "Internet presence sites" provide examples of such new forms of Web-based advertising.

Market orientation operationalizes the "marketing concept," in which firms attempt to uncover and satisfy customer needs at a profit, and refers to the "organization wide generation of market intelligence pertaining to current and future customer needs," along with the dissemination and responsiveness of the organization to such. Kohli and Jaworski suggest that a market orientation will be more related to business performance under conditions of intense competition and unstable market preferences. Since these conditions, along with technological uncertainty, face and will continue to face firms developing new offerings in the

Web for years to come, and since a market orientation can represent a significant competitive advantage for a firm in such cases, it follows that firms interested in Web-based business efforts adopt a market orientation.

Yet, surprisingly, as it is currently evolving, not enough is being done to include the consumer in the development of emerging media. Instead, developments are being driven largely by a one-to-many mass communication model that presumes the growth of a passive mass "audience" rather than heterogenous users seeking varied experiences. But in order to adopt a market orientation, firms must understand their customers and engage in consumer research. However, very little in the way of in-depth consumer research is currently being conducted, perhaps because in information intensive environments, the marketing function is often performed by other functional areas that may not be as familiar with the marketing function as marketers.

The current technological and market turbulence of the Web represents more than mere technological evolution. Thus, we argue that successful Web marketing efforts will require an evolution in the marketing concept to where the firm not only attempts to discover and meet customer needs profitably, but also engages in marketing activities that contribute positively to the development of the emerging medium itself, by developing new paradigms for electronic commerce.

For example, consider a current practice that reflects traditional models. A well known difficulty from a business perspective is that most Web sites have been unable to induce visitors to register, especially when no payment is required to consume content. But if the firm does not know, at a minimum, the characteristics of those visiting its Web site, application of the marketing concept becomes challenging. One proposed solution is to centralize the registration process, collecting demographic and psychographic information from consumers for resale at both the within-site and across-site levels to Web sites interested in linking consumer navigation and transaction behavior with consumer marketing variables.

But a new paradigm constructed from considering the Web as a many-to-many communications medium might suggest decentralizing the registration process so that the consumer retains ownership of his or her personal information and benefits by selling it to commercial Web sites who may desire it. Developing such a concept would not only facilitate registration, but also allow the consumer to participate in and benefit from the process.

In such cases, the role of marketing thus moves from "merely" satisfying customer needs to including an altruistic, cooperative goal of facilitating the development of the market itself, one that explicitly includes the consumer. This is consistent with a recent report by the National Academy of Sciences: "In the new business environment, cooperation may prove more rewarding than competition, and information-sharing more fruitful than information control."

Several propositions from Glazer regarding information intensive marketing environments support our extended marketing concept. Specifically, information leads to "issues of access sharing, and creating opportunities for use." Greater involvement in strategic alliances is proposed to lead to an "extended cooperation framework." Further, in information-intensive environments such as the World Wide Web, attention will be focused less on competitive strategy and more on cooperative strategy.

To a large extent, many of the original structures that were constructed to facilitate electronic commerce on the Web were characteristic of a primitive, simple society, bound by "mechanical solidarity", with a common consciousness and internalized set of shared values. These shared values arose largely from the original core group of Internet users, a relatively homogeneous group of students, academicians, and researchers.

In large part, we believe these origins account for the unwillingness of consumers to register on Web sites and pay for content. However, as the Internet continues to evolve into a complex, heterogeneous virtual society, "organic solidarity" will develop from an increasing interdependence between people pursuing different goals. This produces an increasing division of labor, which will transform existing paradigms and require new rules of cooperation and competition to emerge.

Marketers should focus on playing an active role in the construction of new organic paradigms for facilitating commerce in the emerging electronic society underlying the Web, rather than infiltrating the existing primitive mechanical structures. Consider the nascent attempts by previously proprietary commercial online services to exercise control over both consumer access to the Web and the ability of consumers to provide content to the Web. Increasingly, the commercial online services are becoming consumer gateways to the Web and becoming more like user-friendly Internet Service Providers than closed, proprietary networks.

Yet, as these services reinvent their businesses in the context of many-to-many decentralized open networks, they are beginning to reshape themselves under a broadcast cable model in which a series of Web site selections will be offered to consumers as "channels" easily accessible by a simple point-and-click interface. Web sites not endorsed may be accessible, but would require knowledge of the URL; it would be less likely that consumers would seek out such content.

In some cases, consumers may not even know additional content exists, let alone how to access it. Such attempts, following from the traditional one-to-many mass model of communication effects, obviously do take full advantage of the medium's unique features and hold enormous implications for how the Web will develop as a commercial medium. At the minimum, it implies the development of homogenized content that would appeal to a mass audience, with attendant negative implications for niche or small Web sites lacking mass audience appeal. This erroneous view of the Web as a traditional broadcast medium also largely explains the United States Justice Department's recent efforts to censor "indecent" content on the Internet.

In contrast, the effective marketer will be actively constructing new models for marketing on the Web, based upon an increasingly diverse and complex virtual society. Such efforts will contribute to the establishment of organic solidarity within the heterogeneous market defined by segments of consumers and firms doing business on the Web.

It is still too soon to predict the form these efforts might take, even as the business models emerge. Yet it seems clear that

1) steps to build the infrastructure for electronic commerce;

2) mechanisms that take advantage of the medium's unique features; and

3) attempts to develop stimulating and exciting content-rich sponsored environments, hold tremendous promise toward this goal.

In a recent report on Electronic Enterprises, the Office of Technology Assessment noted that "because exchange transactions will increasingly be carried out electronically and online, the network will in many instances serve as the market." While it has been said for traditional media that "the medium is the message", with the Web it is also true that "the medium is the market."

The establishment of broadly-based, "integrated destination sites" like GNN (www.gnn.com), HotWired (www.hotwired.com), and Pathfinder (www.timeinc.com) support this observation and lead us to argue that as media increase in their interactive and navigational capabilities, they move from serving as communication and marketing channels to serving as markets.

The Internet as a marketplace has the potential to make markets more efficient. This is particularly so for the Web because it offers not only the opportunity to provide full information to consumers about goods and services, but lends itself to rich detail and specificity regarding such information, especially compared to traditional media. There is also greater probability of a well-informed consumer, since the consumer has greater control over the search process. Such control is likely to facilitate a highly developed form of, for example, price comparison shopping. Thus, compared to conventional markets, the cost of information should be lower and the information quality should be higher, leading to a higher degree of market efficiency. Therefore, the market represented by the Web also has the potential to be a more efficient market than conventional markets.

However, before this can occur, the infrastructure must be built. The current difficulty transmitting sensitive data, such as credit card numbers and the like, securely over the Internet is transforming traditional payment processes.

Until secure systems are widely implemented on the Web, the lack of such represents a significant barrier to adoption of the Web for commercial transactions. Thus, new systems must be developed to permit virtual transactions directly over the network. These may take the form of "digital cash" or credit card number encryption, allowing commercial transactions to take place directly rather than through parallel traditional channels.

Equally important will be online dynamic content directories both within a site and across the Web. With over 21 million Web pages indexed by Digital Equipment Corporation's Alta Vista search index as of February 19, 1996, and the number growing daily, efficient ways to help consumers sort and search through the myriad of offerings available will be critical. Research in consumer decision making suggests that, in the absence of heuristics, decision effectiveness degrades in the presence of too much information. Thus, the challenge for marketers will be to develop, in conjunction with consumers, rule-based systems for the organization of content that exploit the principles of network navigation and facilitate flow.

As a distribution channel, the Web possesses

1) extremely low entry and exit barriers for firms;
2) increasing irrelevance of distribution intermediaries; and
3) the capability to not only keep pace with market change, but accelerate it.

Because the Web increases the power of the consumer and decreases the power of the firm, compared to traditional channels of distribution, the consumer and the firm approach "symmetrical power" and the best communication efforts are likely to be "collaborative" rather than "autonomous".

In the presence of higher information intensity, channel power shifts in favor of consumers and a breakdown occurs in formal distinctions between producer and consumer. In the information intensive Web environment, the firm is no longer broadcasting a single communication to many consumers, but in effect tailoring its communications according to consumers' varied interests and needs.

This is currently implemented through the unique process of network navigation in which the consumer chooses what information (if any) to receive from the firm. Thus, marketers must begin to examine the manner in which these more collaborative communication efforts should proceed.

These shifts in channel power hold important implications for consumer participation in the marketing process. For example, consumers may collaborate not only in idea generation and product design, but also in the marketing communication effort itself. This is because interactivity in the Web gives consumers much greater control of the message. Such control may manifest itself in startlingly new ways: for example, it is feasible for consumers interested in purchasing big-ticket durables such as cars or appliances to broadcast their interest and solicit open bids from different firms. Similarly, Digital has enjoyed success with their innovative program of making the Alpha AXP computer systems available to potential customers for "test drive" over the Web.

Such activities are possible because the process of network navigation in the Web is characterized by open access to information. The original motivation for developing an "internetwork" of computers, on which the Web is based, was to enable geographically dispersed computers representing diverse platforms to link and communicate so they could economically share costly resources. The Internet thus developed in a rich and exciting atmosphere of intellectual curiosity fostered in an unconstrained and creative environment.

Marketers can utilize the opportunities for customer interaction inherent in the Web in numerous ways, including

1) the design of new products;
2) the development of product and marketing strategy, and
3) the innovation of content.

The evolution of content on the Web is dependent upon not only the evolution of existing metaphors and communication codes from traditional media, but also new techniques and conventions inherent in the possibilities of the medium itself. One implication of this is that the content that will make the Web commercially successful have likely not been invented yet, and may require more than a simple continuous innovation of existing content.

As evidence that a discontinuous evolution in content will be required to fuel the growth of the Web, witness the difficulties experienced in applying traditional content to the alternative new interactive multimedia. Few applications have yet to meet with consumer acceptance in test markets, and even fewer have come online in any significant way.

The limitations of relying on old paradigms become apparent when we consider the "more is better" logic implicit in current approaches to measuring consumer activity on sponsored content Web sites.

Driven by traditional mass media models, "hit" and visit counting methods implicitly seek to achieve unstated mass audience levels, since in traditional media, "advertising effectiveness" is tied to ratings or circulation models where larger numbers are preferred.

Yet in the Web, advertising effectiveness can be explicitly tied to customer response and the possibility exists of developing new measurement systems that capture the value of a single consumer's visit and subsequent response in new and innovative ways.

New bases for market segmentation will also be needed for Web based marketing efforts because consumers vary in their ability to achieve flow. Research can determine the variables that relate to a consumer's propensity to enter the flow state and such information can be used to develop marketing efforts designed to maximize the chances of the consumer achieving flow. Since "repeat purchase," that is, repeat visits to a particular Web site, will be increased if the environment faciiitates the flow state, the marketing objective on the first visit (i.e. "trial"), will be to provide for these flow opportunities.

Pricing strategy is also relevant here. Commercial online service pricing models are largely based upon connect time and usage charges. Such schemes have the effect of discouraging usage and, increasingly, consumers are demanding flat-rate pricing schemes.

In the short run, flat-rate systems encourage consumer experimentation and system use. Continued use feeds demand because, as the anecdotal record shows, usage tends to be "addicting." This suggests that pricing algorithms that encourage browsing will encourage usage.

The traditional one to many model, with its attendant implications and consequences for marketing theory and practice, has only limited utility in emerging many-to-many media like the World Wide Web, and that a new marketing paradigm is required for this communication medium.

In this paradigm, new rules of cooperation and competition can emerge in which marketers focus on playing an active role in the construction of new standards and practices for facilitating commerce in the emerging electronic society underlying the Web.

The Web as both medium and market is more likely to be successful if it frees consumers from their traditionally passive role as receivers of marketing communications, gives them much greater control over the search for and acquisition of information relevant for consumer decision making, and allows them to become active participants in the marketing process. Firms have the opportunity to reap the benefits of this innovation in interactivity by being closer to the customer than ever before.

Doing business on the Web doesn't spare you from many of the same laws and customs that govern businesses in the physical world. You must pay especially close attention to trademark law, which governs disputes between business owners over the names, logos and trademarks that identify their goods and services in the marketplace. Applied to Web businesses, trademark law determines when the use of a particular Internet domain name infringes someone else's trademark.

The two most fundamental rules of trademark law are:

— You can't use a name, logo or domain name that might confuse customers about the source of your goods or services.

— You can't use a name, logo or domain name that invokes a famous product or service, even if customers wouldn't be confused.

Until several years ago, only companies doing business on a national or regional level needed to be concerned about trademark law. A local business could reasonably expect its marketing activities to be limited to a neighborhood, town, city or county. As long as the name used by the business to identify itself in the marketplace didn't seriously conflict with names used by other local businesses, there was little likelihood of customer confusion and so, little likelihood of legal conflict.

Today, the core concept of "local" has all but disappeared for many types of businesses. When you create a Web page, you enter a commercial realm that is in one stroke local, national and international. Local customers can search you out, but so can anyone anywhere in the U.S. or the world who has a computer and an Internet connection. Suddenly, you must pay attention to how your business name—or the names of products you are offering—fit within the vast sea of names that is the new world marketplace.

The first trademark issue to arise when you create a Web page has to do with the name you give your Web site—called your Internet domain name. It's the unique part of your Internet address (Universal Resource Locator or URL). The Nolo Press URL, for instance, is http://www.nolo.com. The last part—nolo.com—is the domain name. Naturally, most businesses want the domain name for their Web site to be the same as their business name, so that customers can easily find their sites. Here's where you can inadvertently court trademark trouble. If you choose a domain name that is the same or similar to a business name that is already in use as a trademark anywhere in the country (in physical or virtual space), you could find yourself in a trademark infringement dispute. If you are offering goods or services on your website, you could even be sued.

The entity responsible for assigning domain names does not check to see if a requested domain name violates an existing trademark. It is concerned only with whether the name is already taken as a domain name. In other words, being assigned the domain name you request says nothing about whether it will conflict with an existing trademark. If it is the same or similar to a famous mark or is likely to cause customers to confuse your site with the business or products carrying the existing mark, you could be in violation of trademark law. If you do pick a domain name that creates a trademark conflict, you will most likely lose the name. Given the energy that goes into building domain name recognition, this could be a major blow to your business. Here's what could happen:

— If your domain name prevents the owner of a registered trademark from using its mark as its domain name, the owner of the registered mark may be able to cause your domain name to be deregistered. If that happens, you can't use it anymore.

— If your domain name is the same or similar to an existing famous mark, the mark's owner may file a lawsuit preventing any further use of your domain name, even if customers wouldn't likely be confused. For example, if you decide to call your health food website foramazons.com, the real amazon.com could probably force you to stop using the name, simply because it calls amazon.com to mind.

— If your domain name conflicts with an existing mark and will likely lead to customer confusion between your business or products and those offered by the mark's owner, you may be forced to stop using the name. And if your infringement is judged to be willful, you might have to both compensate the mark's owner for any losses and pay thousands of dollars in statutory damages.

Before choosing a domain name, it is wise to conduct what's known as a trademark search. A trademark search hunts for any trademarks, federally registered or not, that conflict with your proposed domain name.

Technically, no two domain names may be exactly the same. But because all businesses use the ".com" extension as part of their domain names, many newcomers to the Web find that the domain name they want has already been claimed. In response to this problem, an International Ad Hoc Committee created by an organization known as the Internet Society has come up with a plan to add seven new extensions:

— .firm, for businesses or firms;
— .store, for businesses selling goods;
— .web, for sites emphasizing activities involving the World Wide Web;
— .arts, for sites emphasizing cultural and entertainment activities;
— .rec, for sites emphasizing recreational entertainment;
— .info, for sites offering information services; and
— .nom, for sites supported by individuals.

With all the attention Amazon.com and other consumer Web sites receive, one would think the big money is in business-to-consumer e-commerce. The real story is that business-to-business e-commerce is a much larger market. Forrester research estimates that b-to-b e-commerce for 1998 was $43 billion, or more than five times b-to-c. What's more, Forrester projects that b-to-b e-commerce will reach $1.3 trillion by 2003. The Aberdeen Group estimates actual b-to-b commerce at ten to twenty times that of b-to-c commerce. A survey by Cahner's Publishing found that "61% of manufacturing professionals have made a purchase as a result of seeing a product or service on the Internet." Their 1998 Internet-influenced purchasing increased 13% from the prior year.

It's very clear that the Internet will not soon be an important part of business-to-business marketing, it already is.

Still, many business sectors have yet to embrace e-commerce. Experts are now estimating the cost of putting together a serious, yet status quo, e-commerce Web site at around $1 million. A cutting edge site is much more costly. Clearly, this has kept many businesses from moving their Web efforts from the realm of brochureware to become a more serious part of their business.

The potential of b-to-b e-commerce to cut costs in the supply chain is significant — in some cases, e-commerce has the potential to eliminate the need for certain channel members completely. E-commerce even allows some manufacturers of consumer products who have traditionally sold to retailers to sell directly to consumers, but this, of course, can greatly upset retailers and others in the value chain.

A recent memo from Home Depot to its retail goods suppliers warned them that if they sell their goods directly on the Internet, Home Depot will stop doing business with them — clearly illustrating some of the temptation and dangers of e-commerce for manufacturers who currently sell to retailers.

Another strong reason why business-to-business e-commerce is certain to grow is its ability to save money for both the buyer and the seller. According to Giga Information Group, by 2002, e-commerce will save businesses $1.25 billion a year (companies saved approximately $17.6 billion in 1998; US companies saved about $15.2 billion). But the real killer for companies not embracing e-commerce may be time. Companies who are late to embrace e-commerce may be ruined by e-commerce savvy competitors. The time it takes to develop and implement e-commerce systems can be lengthy.

A recent example of the consequences of being too late comes from a Fortune 100 manufacturer of consumer electronics. Recently, the manufacturer told its suppliers that if they do not presently have e-commerce capabilities they will soon be eliminated as suppliers. Companies without current e-commerce capabilities didn't even get the chance to adapt — they were blindsided. Why did this manufacturer do this? Because they realized that implementing e-commerce systems is a very long and costly process that can be filled with setbacks — they knew that they would lose potential cost savings in the process. It is certain that traditional value-added network (VAN)-based EDI (Electronic Data Interchange) will soon be replaced by Internet-based EDI.

The cost efficiencies of replacing VAN-based EDI with Internet-based EDI is simply too attractive on too many levels to be ignored. For example, VAN based EDI is cost prohibitive for many small businesses, while Internet-based EDI is relatively inexpensive. Consequently, Internet-based EDI will be the technology that levels the playing field for many small businesses. For many companies, it appears that the largest factors impeding the progress of b-to-b e-commerce are a lack of management commitment, high start-up costs and a lack of technology standards.

3

Electronic Payments

The Internet has taken its place beside the telephone and television as an important part of people's lives. Consumers use the Internet to shop, bank and invest online. Most consumers use credit or debit cards to pay for online purchases, but other payment methods, like "e-wallets," are becoming more common.

Most online shoppers use credit cards to pay for their online purchases. But debit cards - which authorize merchants to debit your bank account electronically - are increasing in use. Your debit card may be an automated teller machine (ATM) card that can be used for retail purchases. To complete a debit card transaction, you may have to use a personal identification number (PIN), some form of a signature or other identification, or a combination of these identifiers. Some cards have both credit and debit features

New electronic payment systems - sometimes referred to as "electronic money" or "e-money" - are also occurring. Their goal is to make purchasing simpler. For example, "stored-value" cards let you transfer cash value to a card. They're commonly used on public transportation, at colleges and universities and at gas stations. Many retailers also sell stored value cards in place of gift certificates. Some stored-value cards work offline, say, to buy a candy bar at a vending machine; others work online, for example, to buy an item from a website; some have both offline and online features. Some cards can be "reloaded" with additional value, at a cash machine; other cards are "disposable" - you can throw them away after you use them. Some stored-value cards contain computer chips that make them "smart" cards: These cards can act like a credit card as well as a debit card, and also can contain stored value.

Some new Internet-based payment systems allow value to be transmitted through computers, sometimes called "e-wallets." You can use "e-wallets" to make "micropayments" - very small online or offline payments for things like a magazine or fast food.

When you buy something using your e-wallet, the balance on your online account decreases by that amount. "E-wallets" may work by using some form of stored value or by automatically accessing an account you've set up through a computer system connected to your credit or debit card account.

Although the consumer can't control fraud or deception on the Internet, he/she can take steps to recognize it, avoid it and report it. Here's how.

— Use a secure browser - software that encrypts or scrambles the purchase information you send over the Internet - to guard the security of your online transactions. Be sure your browser has the most up-to-date encryption capabilities by using the latest version available from the manufacturer. You also can download some browsers for free over the Internet. When submitting your purchase information, look for the "lock" icon on the browser's status bar to be sure your information is secure during transmission.

— Before you provide any personal financial information to a website, check the site's privacy policy. In particular, determine how the information will be used or shared with others and what security features are in place so the information cannot be obtained fraudulently. If you're not comfortable with the policy, consider doing business elsewhere.

— Read and understand the privacy, refund and shipping policies of the websites you visit, before you make your purchase. Look closely at the disclosures about a website's security, its refund and shipping policies and its privacy policy on collecting and using your personal information. Some websites' disclosures are easier to find than others - look at the bottom of the home page, on order forms or in the "About" or "FAQs" section of a site.

— Keep your personal information private. Don't disclose your personal information - your address, telephone number, Social Security number, bank account number or e-mail address - unless you know who's collecting the information, why they're collecting it and how they'll use it.

— Give payment information only to businesses you know and trust, and only when and where it is appropriate - like an order form. Never give your password to anyone online, even your Internet service provider. Do not download files sent to you by strangers or click on hyperlinks from people you don't know. Opening a file could expose your system to a computer virus or a program that could hijack your modem.

— Keep records of your online transactions and read your e-mail. Merchants may sends you important information about your purchases.

— Review your monthly credit card and bank statements for any errors or unauthorized purchases promptly and thoroughly. Notify your credit or debit card issuer immediately if your credit or debit card or checkbook is lost or stolen, or if you suspect someone is using your accounts without your permission.

The US Fair Credit Billing Act (FCBA) and Electronic Fund Transfer Act (EFTA) establish procedures for resolving errors on credit and bank account statements, respectively, including:

— credit charges or electronic fund transfers that you - or anyone you've authorized to use your account - have not made;

— credit charges or electronic fund transfers that are incorrectly identified or show the wrong amount or date;

— computation or similar errors;

— a failure to properly reflect payments or credits, or electronic fund transfers;

— not mailing or delivering credit billing statements to your current address, as long as that address was received by the creditor in writing at least 20 days before the billing period ended; and

— credit charges or electronic fund transfers for which you request an explanation or documentation, because of a possible error.

The FCBA generally applies to "open end" credit accounts - that is, credit cards and revolving charge accounts, like department store accounts. It does not apply to loans or credit sales that are paid according to a fixed schedule until the entire amount is paid back, like an automobile loan.

The EFTA applies to electronic fund transfers - transactions involving automated teller machines (ATMs), debit cards and other point-of-sale debit transactions, and other electronic banking transactions that can result in the withdrawal of cash from your bank account.

Under the EFTA, if there is a mistake or unauthorized withdrawal from consumer's bank account through the use of a debit card, or other electronic fund transfers, consumer must notify the financial institution of the problem or error not later than 60 days after the statement containing the problem or error was sent.

Although most financial institutions have a toll-free number to report the problem, consumer should follow up in writing. For retail purchases, consumer's financial institution has up to 10 business days to investigate after receiving his notice of the error. The error must be corrected within one business day after determining the error has occurred.

The FCBA and the EFTA may not cover stored-value cards or transactions involving them, so consumer may not be covered for loss or misuse of the card. However, stored-value cards still might be useful for micropayments and other small purchases online because they can be convenient and - in some cases - offer anonymity.

Shopping online opens up a whole world of goods and services. With the simple click of a computer mouse, the consumer can order tulip bulbs directly from Holland, exotic spices from Turkey or handwoven wall hangings from Mexico or Morocco. The World Wide Web has expanded the international marketplace in a way never before possible, giving consumers unlimited choices.

But shopping electronically-especially when consumer is dealing with vendors in other countries-opens up a whole world of questions. Are the prices posted in U.S. dollars or some other currency? Does the company ship internationally? How long will it take for an order to be delivered? Will unexpected taxes or duties be added to the price? If there's a problem, where can the consumer get it resolved?

The US Federal Trade Commission offers these tips to help the consumer when he "go global":

— *Know to whom the conusmer is dealing with.* Do some homework to make sure a company is legitimate before doing business with it. Identify the company's name, its physical address, including the country where it is based, and an e-mail address or telephone number, so the consumer can contact the company with questions or problems. And consider dealing only with vendors that clearly state their policies.

— *Know what is buying.* Look for accurate, clear and easily accessible information about the goods or services being offered, and contact the company to clear up any questions before place an order.

— *Understand the terms, conditions and costs involved in the sale.* Find out up front what are getting for money and what are not. Get a full, itemized list of costs involved in the sale, with a clear designation of the currency involved, terms of delivery or performance, and terms, conditions and methods of payment. Look for information about restrictions, limitations or conditions of the purchase; instructions for proper use of products, including safety and health care warnings; warranties and guarantees; cancellation, return, or refund policies; and the availability of after-sale service.

— *Protect when paying online.* Look for information posted online that describes the company's security policies, and check whether the browser is secure and encrypts the personal and financial information during online transmission. That makes the information less vulnerable to hackers.

— *Look out for privacy.* All businesses require information about you to process an order. Some use it to tell customers about products, services or promotions, but others share or sell the information to other vendors—a practice with which you may not be comfortable.

— *Shop only from online vendors that respect privacy.* Look for the vendor's privacy policy on the web site. The policy statement should reveal what personal identifying information is collected about the cosnsumer and how it will be used, and give him the opportunity to refuse having the information sold or shared with other vendors.

— *Understand the recourse.* Do business only with companies that state their commitment to customer satisfaction and their policy to resolve consumer complaints or difficulties quickly and fairly, without imposing excessive charges or inconvenience.

— *Get smart about e-commerce.* Demand consumer friendly policies and procedures. Look for information from businesses, consumer representatives and governments about the rights and responsibilities when participating in international electronic commerce. Take an active role in advancing an electronic marketplace that promotes fair and effective policies and procedures that protect businesses as well as consumers.

Consumers around the world are increasingly turning to their computers to buy a wide array of goods and services. And because the World Wide Web is, as its name implies, worldwide, businesses that sell online can potentially reach billions of customers in every country of the world. Even small "mom-`n-pop" companies with websites are attracting a client base never before possible. Many are discovering just how international the Internet really is, processing orders not only from the next town or state, but from the next continent, too.

That presents new challenges to sellers who have never shipped overseas and may have little experience with the taxes, duties and customs laws involved. It also raises questions about consumer protections. When buying from an overseas vendor, what, if any, protections do consumers have if they run into problems? How safe is it to transmit credit information overseas via the Internet? How long will it take for an order to be delivered? Are unexpected taxes or duties routinely added to the price?

New international guidelines are helping to answer those and other questions. The United States and 28 other countries, working together as members of the Organization for Economic Cooperation and Development, have signed on to new guidelines.

The guidelines:

— set out principles for voluntary "codes of conduct" for businesses involved in electronic commerce;

— offer guidance to governments in evaluating their consumer protection laws regarding electronic commerce; and,

— give consumers advice about what to expect and what to look for when shopping online.

The goal is to build consumer confidence in the global electronic marketplace by working to ensure that consumers are just as safe when shopping online as when shopping offline-no matter where they live or where the company they do business with is based.

E-Businesses that adhere to the guidelines:

— Use fair business, advertising and marketingpractices. They provide truthful, accurate and complete information to consumers, and avoid deceptive, misleading or unfair claims, omissions or practices. The businesses can back up all claims, such as claims about how well a product works or how quickly a product will arrive.

— Provide accurate, clear and easily accessible information about the company and the goods or services it offers. They disclose the information consumers need to understand whom they're dealing with and what they're buying. These businesses post the company's name, its physical address, including the country, and an email address or telephone number consumers can use if they have questions or problems. They also provide a clear, complete description of the product or service being offered. That helps take the guesswork out of online shopping and could reduce the number of complaints filed by dissatisfied consumers after the sale.

— Disclose full information about the terms, conditions and costs of the transaction. They provide consumers a full, itemized list of costs involved in the transaction, designating the currency involved, as well as terms of delivery or performance, and terms, conditions and methods of payment. If applicable and appropriate to a transaction, these businesses also include information about restrictions, limitations or conditions of the purchase; instructions for proper use of the product and any safety and health care warnings; warranties and guarantees; cancellation or refund policies; and whether after-sale service is available. If it's possible to carry out a transaction in more than one language, they make available all important terms and conditions in each language.

— Ensure that consumers know they are making a commitment to buy before closing the deal. These businesses take steps to protect consumers who are merely "surfing" the 'Net from unknowingly entering into a sales contract. They give the consumer a chance to change the order before committing to the purchase or to cancel it altogether.

— Provide an easy-to-use and secure method foronline payments. They adopt security measures appropriate to the transactions to make sure that personal information is less vulnerable to hackers.

— Protect consumer privacy during electronic commerce transactions. They disclose their privacy policies or information practice statements prominently on their websites, and offer people choices about how their personal information is used. They give consumers the opportunity to refuse having their personal information shared with others or used for promotional purposes.

— Address consumer complaints and difficulties. They have policies and procedures to address consumer problems quickly and fairly, and without excessive cost or inconvenience to the consumer. They also take advantage of alternative dispute resolution mechanisms.

— Adopt fair, effective and easy to understand self-regulatory policies and procedures. They extend to electronic commerce the same basic level of protections that cover other forms of commerce. The agreement encourages businesses to work with consumer representatives to develop policies and procedures that give consumers the tools they need to make informed decisions and to resolve complaints.

— Help educate consumers about electronic commerce. They are helping create a consumer-friendly electronic marketplace. These businesses work with governments and consumer representatives to ensure that consumers understand their rights and responsibilities when participating in online commerce.

The guidelines also call on participating governments to take steps to boost consumer confidence in the electronic marketplace. They encourage governments to evaluate their consumer protection laws to make sure they extend to online shopping, and to ensure that consumers have recourse if they are dissatisfied.

And they recommend that governments work together to combat cross-border fraud and help establish a climate for electronic commerce that balances the needs and interests of businesses and consumers.

Internet auctions

Since their first appearance in 1995, Internet auctions have become one of the hottest phenomena of the web. They offer buyers a "virtual flea market" with an endless range of merchandise from around the world — and they give sellers a "storefront" from which to market everything from sports memorabilia to computer systems to millions of international buyers.

Whether you're a buyer or a seller, there's a smart way to "do" Internet auctions. Here's how to make sure you get the most from your auction action.

Internet auctions are bazaars. In most cases, sellers offer one item at a time, but sometimes sellers offer multiple lots of the same item. The auction web sites often refer to auctions of multiple items as "Dutch" or "English" auctions. At some sites, the seller may be required to sell all items at the price of the lowest successful bid. At other sites, the seller is entitled to the prices bid by each of the highest bidders. Occasionally, Internet auction sellers set a "reserve price," which is the lowest price they will accept for an item. Some sites disclose the reserve price during the auction.

The bidding for each auction closes at a scheduled time, when the highest bidder "wins." In the case of sales of multiple lots, the participants with the highest bids at the close of the auction are obligated to buy the items. If no one bids at or above the reserve price, the auction closes without a "winner." At the close of a successful auction, the buyer and seller communicate — usually by e-mail — to arrange for payment and delivery of the goods.

Internet auctions can be business-to-person or person-to-person. Operators of business-to-person auction sites have physical control of the merchandise being offered and accept payment for the goods. In person-to-person auctions, individual sellers or small businesses offer their items for auction directly to consumers. Generally, the seller — not the site — has physical possession of the merchandise. After the auction closes, the seller is responsible for dealing directly with the highest bidder to arrange for payment and delivery.

Buyers may have several payment options, including credit card, debit card, personal check, cashier's check, money order, cash on delivery and escrow services. However, all sellers do not accept all forms of payment.

Credit cards offer buyers the most consumer protections, including the right to seek a credit from the credit card issuer if the product is not delivered or if the product received isn't the product ordered. Typically, sellers using business-to-person auction sites accept payment by credit card. But many sellers in person-to-person auctions don't. Usually they require payment by cashier's check or money order before they send the item to the winning bidder.

Some sellers agree to use an escrow service. For a fee — generally 5 percent of the cost of the item, paid by the buyer — an escrow service accepts payment from the buyer via check, money order or credit card. The service releases the money to the seller only after the buyer receives and approves the merchandise. This helps protect buyers from ending up empty-handed after paying their money. Using an escrow service can delay the deal. With any business transaction, investigate the service's reputation before signing on to the service.

According to the Federal Trade Commission, Internet auction fraud has become a significant problem. Most consumer complaints center on sellers who:

— don't deliver the advertised goods;

— deliver something far less valuable than they advertised;

— don't deliver in a timely way; or

— fail to disclose all the relevant information about the product or terms of the sale.

If You're A Buyer:

— Identify the seller and check the seller's feedback rating.

— Do your homework. Be sure you understand what you're bidding on, its relative value and all terms and conditions of the sale, including the seller's return policies and who pays for shipping.

— Establish your top price and stick to it.

— Evaluate your payment options. If possible, use a credit card. It offers the most protection if there's a problem. Consider using an escrow service if the seller doesn't accept credit cards.

Know the Seller

— Find out who you're dealing with. Verify the seller's identity before you place your bid, and be wary of sellers who you can't identify. Some sellers may use a forged e-mail header, which makes follow-up contact close to impossible.

— Get a telephone number for the seller and use it to confirm that you have some way other than e-mail to contact the seller.

— Check to see how the seller has treated other buyers. Some auction sites post feedback ratings of sellers based on comments by other buyers. This may give you some idea of how you'll be treated, but beware of "shill" testimonials.

— Before you bid, find out what form of payment the seller will accept. If the seller accepts only cashier's checks or money orders, decide whether you are willing to take the risk of sending your payment before you receive the product.

— Find out who pays for shipping and delivery. Generally, sellers specify the cost of shipping the item and give buyers the option of express delivery for an additional fee. If you're uncertain about shipping costs, check with the seller before you bid.

— Check on the seller's return policy. Can you return the item for a full refund if you're not satisfied with it? If you return it, are you required to pay shipping costs or a restocking fee?

— If you have any questions about the item, e-mail or phone the seller. Don't place your bid until your questions have been answered.

Know the Product

— When considering whether to place a bid, know exactly what you're buying. Read the seller's description of the item or service, and if a photograph is posted, take time to look at it closely.

— Try to determine the relative value of an item before you bid. There's no guarantee that something is a good deal just because it's on the Internet auction block. "Brick-and-mortar" stores and online price-trading sites may be good reality checks on price. If you find a bargain at an auction site, remember the adage about deals that seem too good to be true. They usually are.

— Read the fine print. Look for words like "refurbished," "close-out," "discontinued" or "off-brand," especially when shopping for computer gear or electronic equipment.

— Consider whether the item comes with a warranty, and where you'll get follow-up service if you need it. Many sellers don't have the expertise or facilities to provide services for the goods they sell. If that's the case with your seller, be sure you're willing to forfeit that protection before placing a bid.

Know the Auction Site

— Check how the auction works. Don't assume that the rules used by one Internet auction site apply to another. Some sites offer step-by-step tutorials that take potential buyers through the bidding process. Taking a few minutes to go through the tutorial might save you frustration or disappointment later.

— Find out what protections the auction site offers buyers. Some sites provide free insurance or guarantees for items that are undelivered, inauthentic or just not what the seller claimed.

Bidding

— If you decide to enter the bidding, proceed with caution. Establish your top price and stick to it.

— Don't bid on an item you don't intend to buy. Remember that if you're the highest bidder, you are obligated to follow through with the transaction. Auction companies often bar "non- paying bidders" — those who back out of a deal — from future bidding.

— When bidding, take steps to protect your privacy. Don't give out personal identifying information like your Social Security number, driver's license number or bank account number. No seller should need it.

— Save all your transaction information. Print or make note of the seller's identification, the item description and the time, date and price you bid on the item. Print and save a copy of every e- mail you send or receive from the auction company or the seller.

Wrapping Up the Deal

— After you receive an e-mail with news that you've "won" an auction, arrange to pay for your purchase. Pay with a credit card, if possible, but it's likely that the seller will require payment by certified check or money order.

— If you're not comfortable sending a certified check or money order to the seller, consider using an escrow service or paying for your item cash on delivery.

If You're A Seller...

— Provide an accurate description of the item you're selling, including all terms of the sale and who will pay shipping costs.

— Respond quickly to any questions bidders may raise during the auction.

— Contact the high bidder as soon as possible after the auction closes to confirm details of the sale.

— Ship the merchandise as soon as you receive payment.

Your Legal Obligations

— Federal laws prohibit deceptive or misleading acts in commerce, including Internet auctions. You are required to advertise your product or service and the terms of the sale honestly and accurately.

— Sellers are prohibited from placing "shill" bids or false testimonials. Some sellers improperly create a fake identity and bid on their own auctions to drive up the offers. Likewise, some sellers place glowing testimonials about themselves in the comment section of Internet auction sites. These practices are not only unethical, they're also fraudulent.

— Sellers are prohibited from offering illegal goods through Internet auctions. While many auction sites monitor their sites and attempt to delete illegal items, the ultimate responsibility for ensuring that a sale is legal rests with the seller and buyer. Some auction sites post a list of prohibited items as a guide.

— After the auction closes, sellers are required to ship the merchandise within the time frame designated during the auction or, if no time frame is specified, within 30 days. If you can't meet the shipping commitment, you must give the buyer an opportunity to cancel the order for a full refund or agree to the new shipping date.

Advertising Your Product

— Describe your item or service — and its condition — as fully and accurately as possible, including whether it's new, used or reconditioned.

— Anticipate questions buyers might have and try to answer them in the description of your item or service. When possible, include a photograph of the item. The saying about a picture being worth 1,000 words rings especially true in Internet auctions.

— When putting an item up for auction, set the minimum bid at the lowest fair price you're willing to accept. Specify who will pay for shipping, and add whether you'll ship internationally.

— State your return policy in your auction description, and if you require the buyer to pay shipping costs or restocking fees for returns. Tell bidders where to get follow-up service. If you don't provide service for the item, say where the bidder could get it.

The Art of the Deal

— If a bidder asks a question about the item you're selling or the sales terms, respond as quickly as possible.

— When the auction closes, print all the information about the transaction, making a note of the buyer's identification, the description of the item and the time, date and price of the bid. Print and save a copy of every e-mail you send and receive from the auction site or successful bidder.

— Contact the winning bidder as quickly as possible after the auction closes. That's the time to confirm the final cost, including shipping charges, and to tell the buyer where to send the payment.

— Most sellers in person-to-person auctions require buyers to pay by check or money order because they don't have the capability to accept credit card payments. These payment methods offer fewer consumer protections than credit cards, so be aware that some buyers may not be comfortable using them. Some online auctions and third parties enable sellers to accept credit card payments. Review the terms of these offers carefully. If you accept credit card payments, bill the buyer's credit card account only when you're ready to ship the product.

4

Wireless Application Protocol

According to the advertisements appearing in magazines of late its possible to receive and send email in the back of a cab, check stocks and share markets while walking down the street and even book flight tickets en route to the airport. In theory it should soon be feasible to arrive in a foreign city armed only with a cell phone and not only find your way around, but also locate branches of your favorite department stores, find a place to stay and even a café or bar and someone suitable to invite for a drink.

The reality of these claims is an expensive and time-consuming experiment into data transfer through the airwaves - or if you prefer, waiting an inordinate amount of time to get access to a fraction of the information available from a PC through a mobile phone. But put into context, this is a pretty impressive feat considering the only piece of equipment involved is a six inch piece of plastic with no wires to connect it to any regular network. Wireless Application Protocol (WAP) has made our reliance on phone jacks and cables a thing of the past, if the hype is to be believed. The way WAP works is similar to making a regular call from a cell phone. The data being sent and received from the unit is carried as a digital signal across the airwaves, so far in approach to a normal call. Once the data is received by a cell phone transmitter it is sent to a server machine run by the network provider. This server is connected to the Internet like a regular PC server but it also plays host to a WAP gateway.

The gateway is in effect a piece of software that strips all of the formatting and graphics from the web page by converting the HTML (Hypertext Markup Language) code of the site to WML (Wireless Markup Language). This WML code is then sent via the wireless network back to the mobile unit, which then displays the text on the cell phone screen.

This access is limited at best and is restricted to specially designed WAP-friendly sites or those that have no pictorial links (which cannot be converted to WML). As a result many sites are inaccessible to the system and so only a fraction of the facilities provided by the Internet can be accessed in this way. Although countless firms are waiting until clear benefits are visible before taking the next step, some organizations are investing in parallel WAP-friendly sites.

WAP enables users to view the latest news headlines and sports results, keep an eye on the stock market and check their bank balances, all while on the move. Plus there are plenty of improvements on the cards: BT Cellnet has already been carrying out trials of a nation-wide General Packet Radio Service (GPRS) system, which will offer a constant connection to the internet at significantly higher speeds than current GSM system can provide. A similar system 'i-mode', already in place in

Japan, shows the effect that a GPRS system could have in the UK. The i-mode system attracted over a million subscribers in its first month, and reached 14 million by November 2000. This is projected to reach 60 million by 2002.

The major UK mobile telecoms providers have paid £22.5 billion for the licenses required to run these so called 3G (Third Generation) services, making it clear that they see the next generation of phones taking off in a huge way, all heading towards the Universal Mobile Telephone System (UMTS).

The number of WAP phones in use in Western Europe at the start of 2001 was around 7 million. This is set to rise to around 50 million by 2004. The WAP is an emerging industry standard whose goal is to provide wireless internet-like services and information to handheld devices that have limited display and data capabilities, such as pagers, cell phones, and Personal Digital Assistants (PDAs).

WAP recognises that the consumer not only values the power and usefulness of the web but also wishes to have it available while away from home or work. WAP consists of wireless equivalents of HTTP and HTML. The HTTP-like component defines the communication protocol between the handheld device and a server or a gateway. This component addresses characteristics that are unique to wireless devices, such as data rate and round-trip response time. The HTML- like component defines new mark-up and scripting languages for displaying information to and interacting with the user. This component is highly focused on the limited display size and limited input devices available on small, handheld devices.

The basic model for WAP is that of the web—a user makes a request for information using a Universal Resource Locator (URL). The URL may be presented to the user in the form of a hyperlink. The information is retrieved and presented to the user. Thus, at either end of the WAP system is a user and a content. The user employs a WAP-compatible client device to make requests and view the content.

Two scenarios are presently envisioned for getting the content to the user. In the first scenario, the client device is in direct communication with a WAP server. In this case, the client device requests the content from a WAP server which retrieves it either locally or remotely and returns it to the device.

In the second scenario, the client device is in communication with a WAP gateway. In this case, the client device request, the content from the gateway which retrieves the content, reformats it, and returns it to the device. WAP provides three broad categories of functionality for content providers: content, scripting and telephony.

The basic display unit of WAP content is a card. A card can be thought of as one screen of information or one part of a fill-in form. In reality, though, a card can span several client device screens since the client device can have a single-line display. It is then up to the client device to determine how to present the entire card as a single entity using scrolling. A card can display text, images, hyperlinks, and input fields, input fields can be fill-in-the-blank type, multiple-choice selections, or buttons. The client device must decide how to render these input fields, how the user navigates between the fields, and how the user enters data into or selects these fields. Since several cards may be required for a single application or service, WAP defines a content file as a group of cards, called a deck. A deck has one or more cards and each card can be labelled, just like name references within HTML files. When a deck is retrieved, the first card is, automatically displayed unless otherwise specified in a reference field of the URL.

The Wireless Mark-up Language (WML) is the scripting language of WAP. WML script is created by a content provider and is stored in its own file, separate from the WML that uses. With WML script, a card can be execute functions that verify input fields or that convey limited state information between cards in a deck or even between decks. WML script are just like functions within other high level languages. WML script functions are invoked by name, can accept parameters, and can return values. They can execute other WML script functions, either in the same file or in another file, and they can execute system library functions to display input fields or to static text.

The telephony control aspects of WAP are much less mature than other aspects of WAP. Since it is expected that WAP will be implemented within a cellphone or other communication devices, it has provisions for controlling the telephony aspects of these client devices. For example, a user may wish to find a local restaurant. Using a WAP cellphone, the user consults the yellow pages of a directory and finds an appropriate place for dinner. To make a reservation, the user just clicks a button displayed by the WML card, and the phone dials the restaurant.

The WAP architecture follows the OSI layering model and consists of three major layers: application layer—WAE and WTA—session layer: WSP and WTLS and Transport layer—WTP and bearer service. The Wireless Application Environment (WAE) and Wireless Telephony Application (WTA) are the topmost layers in the WAP architecture. They are the main interfaces to the client devices and specify a markup language, a scripting language, and a telephony interface. WAE and WTA impose a few, simple, and basic requirements on the client device. WAE consists of WML, WML script and WML script virtual machine.

The Wireless Mark-up Language (WML) is the markup language for WAP-WAE. It is the WAP equivalent of HTML. WML formalises the concept of cards and decks. Much like HTML, WML uses tags, such as 'and', to identify the purpose and function of blocks of text so that the client device can properly display or render them to the user. WML is based on HTML and is also heavily influenced by HDML, used in the Unwired Planet product. WML is XML-compliant and is specified using a full document type definition (DTD). DTD allows a WML text file to be intelligently parsed and verified for correctness.

WML script is the scripting language for WAP-WAE. It is the WAP equivalent of JavaScript. WML Script is a high-level language that allows a content provider to implement arbitrary functions that may be required by individual WML decks. As with WML, WML script is quite verbose and a compression/compilation scheme is defined to make transmission much more efficient. WML script obviously requires an operating environment where the byte codes are executed in an interpreted mode. This virtual machine is similar to the JVM (Java virtual machine).

The Wireless Telephony Application (WTA) is a separate stand-alone function. WTA provides a set of functions that allow control over the client device assuming it is a telephone device. Calls may be placed or answered.

The Wireless Session Protocol (WSP) and the Wireless Transport Layer Security (WTLS) are the session layers of the WAP architecture. They provide connection-based services to the application layer—WAE and WTA. Basically a session is started content is exchanged and the session is later closed. Additionally the session can be suspended and resumed. However, it should not be forgotten, that, although one would think that WTLS belongs in the transport layer, WAP places it in the session layer since the security context is based on WAP sessions rather than WAP transmissions. WSP is the WAP equivalent of HTTP and is based on HTTP/1.1. Within HTTP and WSP is the concept of a request and a reply, each consisting of a header and body. The header is metadata—data about the data—and consists of name-value pain that specify information about the particular request or response. The body is the payload for the WAE/WTA layer and typically consists of tokenised WML, compiled WML script, or images, but can also contain raw WML text. WSP can convey multipart data consisting of several header-data pairs.

Wireless Transport Layer Security (WTLS): WTLS is the WAP equivalent of the HTTP SSL or TLS. Security is provided using encryption of all session data using a cryptographic technique that is negotiated when the connection is established.

The Wireless Transport Protocol (WTP) and bearer services are the protocol layer in the WAP architecture.

They provide reliable transmission of WSP data packets between the client and server over a wireless link. WTP is the WAP equivalent of TCP or UDP. Although WTP should provide reliable communication to WSP, the current specification allows for reliable (TCP-like) or unreliable (UDP-like) communication. When the connection is unreliable, WSP is, unfortunately, responsible for retransmission to make the connection reliable. WTP is responsible for packet segmentation and reassembly and for acknowledgement of packets and retransmission of lost, unacknowledged, or corrupted packets. WTP numbers packets so that an at-most-once policy is effected. This ensures that a retransmitted packet is not mistaken for a new packet, which would cause duplication. The bottom end of WTP consists of adaptation, elements that match WTP functionality to the underlying bearer service, such as SMS or CDPD.

WAP is based heavily on existing web technologies, such as HTML, HTTP, JavaScript, and SSL. The greatest obstacle that WAP faces is market acceptance. In 1960s infotech was limited to institutions, industries, and R&D, Though Total Cost of Ownership (TCO) went up considerably, infotech nevertheless helped to meet the crucial objective of safeguarding the industry. The Indian entrepreneur then only had the option of importing a relevant information technology, which became obsolete by the time it was installed, as the import procedures were cumbersome and time-taking. Profit came from domestic market sales and there was no scope for export. During 1970s, when infotech began to take roots in India, some Chief Executive Officers (CEOs) decided to install computers. These were second-generation systems that were already being replaced abroad by third-generation machines. Investments in business were conventionally decided on the basis of Return on Investment (ROI) and vendors recommended this traditional method. Chief executives had no option but to continue an expensive and an unpopular department, which made no significant contribution to profit.

Perhaps computerisation of activities like financial accounting, payroll, invoicing, and inventory accounting at all levels would have yielded more profit. Computerisation then only implied mechanisation of clerical work or manual processes that involved expenses many times more than cost reduction. Marginal savings could be achieved by improving follow-up on disposal of obsolete items and sundry debtors, but no one figured out even faintly that it was possible to save money through MIS reports' accurate and up-to-date figures. Production planning and control, and design and development were severely handicapped by the inability to carry out calculations fast and were very rudimentary. The installation of computers achieved many things at one stroke.

The compilation of mission-critical data and its subsequent dissemination came under the control of one person. Consistency, accuracy, speed, and detail were assured. The spread of infotech has accelerated in the last ten years, mostly in the medium and large organisations. This technology has brought in its own culture, which must modify the existing culture. This new infotech culture demands discipline. Infotech is expensive and requires expenditure to support infrastructure. It therefore leads to an overall increase in cost. This has to be compensated by increased output of individuals. The pressure on workers therefore increases. Infotech impacts the value systems as well.

In India, WAP is likely to be accepted and nurtured by big corporate houses, as they are in a position to appreciate and assimilate the business benefits of mobile applications much faster. Using portable cellphone-like gadgets that make travel seem like an extension of your desktop life, you can now choose to carry along the power of computers and connectivity even as you travel on a cruiser or jog around the park.

The WAP attempts to set an open standard for wireless protocols, independent of vendor and airlink. It provides a much-needed medium to connect in a secure, fast, nimble, online, interactive way with services, information and other users. It is described as an open, global specification that allows mobile users with wireless devices to easily access and interact with information and services instantly. There are an estimated 380 million mobile phone users as compared to 200 million PCs. By year 2003, mobile phone users are expected to reach at least 1 billion or one out of every six people. Even cynical pundits admit that about 80 per cent of digital handsets shipped by mid-2001 will be WAP-capable.

The wireless hardware world is extremely varied and is innovating virtually every day. Popular devices include the Palm series, Handspring's VisorDeluxe, HP's Jornada series, the Blackberry series, Timeport, Cassiopeia, Compaq's Aero series, Hitachi's HPW series, and so on. Such a critical mass and choice also shrieks for a single standard. All these years, the pace of technology adoption, always the ponderous bug in the digital soup, has been slowed by the low volumes and a general lack of standards in making hand-held products internet compatible. WAP provides the de facto global open standard for wireless data services. The standard is sustained by the WAP Forum, an industry association that now includes hundreds of members. Most of the members have pitched in to develop the world standard for wireless information and telephony services on digital mobile phones and other wireless terminals. The Forum networks with standard-setting bodies like the World Wide Web Consortium (W3C), the European Telecommunication Standards Institute (ETSI), the Telecommunications Industry Association (TIA), the Internet Engineering Task Force (IETF) and the European Computer Manufacturers' Association (ECMA). The primary goal of the WAP Forum is to bring together companies from all segments of the wireless industry value chain.

As with other waves of technology, the success of wireless, too, leans heavily on the availability of applications. Applications will depend on the imagination of business and product managers, and on the creativity of software developers. Significantly, all the pieces necessary for an explosion of applications are now in place. And obliging security vendors have come up with ingenious solutions. Content authoring vendors and tool suppliers offer wireless markup language (WML) as an option. While there were oceans of electronic data held in databases in the pre-internet era, we can now get easy access to structured information and even easier access to their metadata and layouts from anywhere. There are even content conductors, in the form of portal solutions. An example is the enterprise portal, which plays the crucial role of content aggregator, formatter and switch. The server combines the functions of acquiring, securing and intelligently distributing content to various users on demand.

Wireless applications clearly have a major role to play in easing business processes in every situation where information exchange is a critical need. WAP is being used to develop enhanced forms of existing applications and new versions of today's emerging applications. Vendors keen on stretching their application bandwidth are gearing up to make it easier for you to stay wired without wires, so that you can commute, compute, collaborate, converse and confabulate on the run. Existing mobile data software and hardware suppliers are adding WAP support to their offering, either by developing their own WAP interface or, more typically, teaming up with one of the increasing number of WAP gateway providers. WAP allows one to respond to incoming information on the phone by offering you new, easy-to-use menus to access mobile services. This is part of the business case for network operators: by making the value-added services supremely convenient to reply to and request from, WAP can help generate additional traffic and thus, additional revenue. WAP facilitates easy migration of applications between networks and bearers. It resembles Java in the ability to simplify application development. WAP is useful for customer care and servicing from anywhere, message notification and call management, E-mail, telephony value-added services and unified messaging, geographical mapping and locator services, weather and traffic alerts, news, sports and information services, e-commerce transactions and banking services, online address books, directory services, web browsing, document-image-audio sharing and corporate intranet applications.

WAP is not the only version of wireless data transfer. While it has become standard throughout

Europe, the US has its own version, HDML (Handheld Device Markup Language). Though not greatly technologically dissimilar, the primary difference between the two is the ownership right: WAP is a freely-held, or open, standard contrasting to Phone.com's HDML. Switching to the former would reduce divisions and introduce a global standard, but would cost HDML service providers in the replacement of outdated or incompatible equipment.

But the hype behind WAP cannot resolve the difficulties and reservations the everyday user faces when considering their phone bill. When it costs $4 and 10 minutes to send an email or takes half an hour to book tickets for the latest John Woo, many users will simply use alternative technologies. Why bother with the Internet when it would be cheaper, quicker and easier to call, using the primary function of the cell phone.

Current technology allows for a wireless download rate of around 10 kilobits per second. Compare this to the standard 56 kilobits for a wired modem and the difference in speed, and thus cost of access, is clear. With a screen of between two and five lines, and no graphical display or animation, the visual element of the Internet is also lost in the transition between cyberspace and the cell phone.

Such disadvantages don't seem to bother the 10 million iMode cell phone owners in Japan. Since its release in February 1999, the email-phone has made parent telecommunications company NTT DoCoMo the leading Internet service provider in the country.

Statistics seem to indicate that the relatively cheap call costs (around 20 cents to make a quick call and a penny to send an email) have promoted this communication medium in the Far East. Conversely, the prohibitively high cost per call to send the messages have made their American counterparts think twice. Indeed in Finland and Sweden, where cell phone-saturation reaches 66.7% and 57.8% respectively the call charges are the lowest anywhere in the world.

Whatever the criticisms of current wireless technology, its successor is only a mouse click away. Already many mobile communication firms are developing and hyping their version of third generation (3G) technologies. Of course, with all of these different companies competing for prominence it seems as if a global standard for 3G devices will be a long time coming. But when they arrive - as they finally must - the 3G devices may mean science fiction comes to life.

In Douglas Adams' "Hitchhiker's Guide to the Galaxy", the guide is a portable, wireless device which calculates the user's location and displays information about the area. Already offered in a rudimentary form by several European telecommunication firms, the 3G developers promise a more accurate location and extended data access capabilities. Current technology allows placement to around 200 metres in cities and 1.2 kilometres in rural areas. Future devices may lower this distance to a couple of metres no matter where you are. Until 3G arrives though, portable web browsers are doomed to be expensive, slow and maybe not worth the effort.

5

E-Commerce Solutions

The Internet has created an environment that makes that statement truer than at any prior point. The Internet enables incredibly fast access to an enormous amount of information and provides connectivity and community that can empower buyers. According to a popular branding theory, when marketplace choices increase, buyers tend to have an increased preference for familiar brands, thus, saving them research time and limiting their exposure to risk. The Internet has, without question, increased the amount of choices for business-to-business buyers.

Buyers increased access to information often results in increased expectations. In markets where products and services are largely perceived as commodities, or strong weight is given to technical specifications and price, given that all other things are equal, a strong brand may be the single characteristic that differentiates a product from competitive offerings. The significance of geography, which had once created advantages for many companies and obstacles to others, has, in many instances, been greatly reduced. Customers can now quickly and easily research product information, detailed specifications, experience computer-based presentations, search competitor offerings, find peers through professional associations or affinity groups where they can ask questions and share experiences, as well as make purchases online.

There's an old saying in the advertising world: "Nothing kills a bad product faster than good advertising." With the mainstream adoption of the commercial Internet, the time it takes to kill poor or undifferentiated products (for the sake of simplicity, this chapter uses the term "products" to describe both products and services) has been shortened considerably. Innovations are quickly imitated by competitors, rarely providing long-term sustainable advantages. It is clear that the most sustainable advantage any company can have is a strong brand.

Customers now found access to seemingly endless amounts of information results in their being more demanding than prior to this access. While image remains significant, the new access to information often results in placing increased weight on specifications, capabilities and price during the buying process. This complex situation may appear to lessen the significance of brands, but, in actuality, it has elevated the significance of the brand.

Over the last few years, e-commerce has become the buzzword of the business and the finance communities. As a result, more and more companies are jumping into the Internet and e-commerce for fear of being left behind. Boards are directing CEO's to get e-commerce initiatives going and to get them going fast. In a lot of cases the problem is management does not have a clear understanding of what e-commerce is, and how it is different from traditionai bricks and mortar commerce.

E-commerce sites can be divided into two basic types: business to consumer (B2C) and business to business (B2B). In the first wave of e-commerce solutions, companies such ToysRus and a raft of clothing retailers, focused on turning their retail operations into B2C e-commerce operations. In the more recent second wave of e-commerce activity, companies have begun to look at how they can use e-commerce to sell or buy goods from other businesses. Recent initiatives include the recent announcement by Ford and General Motors of their intent to handle all procurement through a joint B2B site and sites like eSteel.

Elements of a B2C e-commerce solution

— *Web browser*: well known software on the consumers' computer that allows them to connect to the WWW and use the standard encryption software (SSL) to shop securely

— *Secure web server*: basic server software that allows a web site to serve information to and collect information from users without risk of the information being stolen (uses SSL)

— *Database engine*: a piece of software or collection of files that organize and store product and customer information for easy retrieval and management

— *Storefront software*: the visual elements to a store and the software that allows the user to choose what products to look at and buy

— *Shopping Cart*: a piece of software that keeps track of the items that customers are interested in buying. Generally includes functionality for adding, removing, reviewing, taxing and paying for products

— *Credit Card Validation Software*: a set of software and connections to the financial institutions that provide the store with the ability to verify and charge items to credit cards. These solutions are can be either real time - i.e. verification and charging takes place while the customer is 'in' the store - or batch processing - i.e. where the credit cards are verified and charged later.

— *Order Tracking and Fulfillment System* : a method of tracking the orders in the database and processing them through a standard procedure to ensure that they are filled.

B2C e-commerce Order Flow

The order flow and site functionality for B2C e-commerce sites can be broken down three ways – taking the order, processing the payment, and fulfilling the order. The process of taking an order through a B2C e-commerce system is very similar to the process in traditional stores. In the following narrative, the traditional action that corresponds to the e-commerce action appears in parentheses.

— the shopper visits the company web site (goes to the store),

— the site now creates a shopping cart for the user that follows with the user throughout the store

— some sites collect customer information and allow users to login to restore preferences and shopping carts even after they have left the store and returned

— the shopper searches for the products they want by clicking through store pages or using a search engine provided by the store site (browses the shelves or gets a sales staff to find an item for them),

— each time a user browses or searches, the storefront software asks the database to provide the information that matches the search criteria

— browsing is actually a set of predefined searches that make sense in the context of the store

— searching allows the user quick access to a specific item or a type of item outside of the browse functions

— the shopper puts the desired items in their shopping cart (same),

— system records information about item into shopping cart (generally contained in the database)

— the shopper reviews shopping cart (heads to checkout),

— e-commerce system provides a list of all items in the cart

— calculates tax on items and provides total

— user able to remove items, proceed to checkout, or continue shopping

— the shopper chooses a shipping option (generally not required for walk in shopping),

— system collects and records shipping information

— system determines cost and displays

— user proceeds to payment (user takes out wallet)

— storefront software switches to secure mode if not already and transfers user to payment processing system.

At this point, the e-commerce store moves into payment processing functionality,

— user provides payment and customer information (pays for items),

— storefront software collects and records customer information

— storefront collects payment information, and may or may not record

— if real time validation is used, credit card validation software communicates with banking institution or credit card portal service

— if real time validation is used, credit card validation software receives verification of validity of card / sufficient funds from financial institution

— if card passes, validation information is recorded in database related to customer shopping cart (which becomes the customer order)

— if card fails, software displays error to user and provides option of trying another card

— if batch validation is used, credit card information is recorded to the database and the user is thanked for their order

— customer leaves store (same)

The fulfillment process

Once an order has been accepted and payment processed, the e-commerce site turns to fulfillment. The fulfillment process is either an issue of picking and shipping the product, or for sites that use just in time procurement, the fulfillment process is the ordering and (drop)shipping of the product.

— e-commerce stores provide means for fulfillment staff to review orders (stocking or special ordering)

— if an e-commerce solution is carrying stock, the e-commerce system will either be the fulfillment system or should at least tie into the legacy fulfillment system at the warehouse

— reports in the fulfillment system will allow the staff to track an order through various stages, which could include ordered (for drop shipping), received (for back ordered stock), shipped/filled

— e-commerce store picks the stock and packs for shipment

— system may need to print packing lists and mailing labels

— advanced fulfillment systems will include an inventory system that will track availability of stock and reflects this availability in the e-commerce site

— e-commerce store arranges for shipping of purchased goods

— store will need to arrange to ship the goods in the method indicated in the customer order

— some fulfillment systems will link into a shipping company system and pickup will be automated to happen as soon as a shipment is marked as filled in the e-commerce fulfillment system

— for e-commerce stores who drop ship purchased goods, the system - increasingly through B2B e-commerce solution - or staff notifies the supplier and marks order filled when confirmation of shipment is received

— orders can be transmitted via a B2B e-commerce solution, fax, phone, or other direct links to suppliers

— the e-commerce will need to get a receipt of shipment from supplier and update the customer order status

— in some jurisdiction, credit cards cannot be charged until goods are actually shipped

Implementation

While the actual implementation of a particular site may not include all aspects discussed, and the implementation may be more or less robust, the general technology and functionality will be present. If a site has lower volumes, the e-commerce solution generally provides limited functionality for fulfillment and shipping integration. The high volume site will have more advanced system.

Elements of B2B e-commerce

The basic technical elements of a B2B e-commerce solution are the same as a B2C solution with the following potential additions:

— *Tender management system*: A tender management system is a system that allows businesses looking to purchase goods/services to issue digital tenders. The tenders will include the descriptions of goods/ services required, date/time, price (optional), quality requirements, and any other miscellaneous terms such as shipping and payment terms.

— *Bid management system*: A bid management system is a system that allows the suppliers on the system to respond to tenders with the appropriate details for their bids. The data collected will depend on the type of B2B system, but will include goods/services offered, date/time available for delivery, price, quality issues, and other miscellaneous terms.

— *Email facilities*: Email facilities will be used in a number of different areas, including bulk mailing for supplier lists and responses/negotiations between a purchaser and supplier. As a result of the sensitive nature of the bidding process, a secure version of the email system may have to be provided (encrypted).

— *Online negotiation system*: The online negotiation system (if present) will be a live chat method that allows two parties to discuss a tender/bid pair securely online. This may include support for a round table discussion of a tender or may instead be handled via teleconferencing outside the system.

— *Contracts issuing system*: The contracts issuing system is an extension to a basic B2B system that allows the participants to issue digitally signed contracts and to store/manage these contracts online. This aspect of the B2B system may be handled instead offline.

— *Electronic Funds Transfer (EFT) system*: The EFT system is a bank to bank transfer system that allows the two parties of a transaction to settle the transaction through a direct withdrawal and deposit system.

— *Digital certificate system for user authentication*: Digital certificates that definitely establish a user's ID may be used in addition to username/password systems in order to provide greater security to B2B sites. These certificates are becoming more common as B2B systems transact higher dollar value transactions.

Great B2B brands have the right technical specifications, connect with customers, deliver on promises that matter, exceed expectations and have a positive buzz within the buying community. Consider the popular mantra of IT professionals: "No one ever got fired for buying IBM." This is a good example of a brand that stands for quality in the minds of customers and provides them with a shortcut in the buying process that helps them avoid risk.

The ideal brand connects with customers on an emotional level. Think B2C brands are the only ones that do this? Consider commercial photographers and Kodak; graphic and multimedia designers and Macintosh; business executives and recruiters and Harvard Business School; computer professionals and IBM; and mechanics and Snap-On.

Smart B2B brands use the Internet to deepen emotional bonding between the brand and customer. These marketers will often create places customers can go online that help encourage their bonding where they can find out more information about the brand, communicate with other brand advocates and feel a sense of a community that is connected by the brand. Microsoft is excellent at creating emotional bonds with the developer community through its various developer groups. These groups have their own special sections of the Microsoft Website, training (including some at no cost), special access to information (they can receive advance notification of announcements prior to the general public), membership, online events such as seminars, discounts on Microsoft products (software and books) plus offline meetings and events.

Microsoft understands how to meld the offline and online worlds together for the benefit of its brand. During the dot-com explosion, the Internet became so over-hyped it seemed that many people had lost touch with (or never understood) sound business principles. Huge amounts of cash were spent in a mad rush to be first to create strong brands in "Internet Speed." Now, long after the Internet bubble has burst, in many instances, there has been a reactionary backlash —a tendency to discount all things related to the Internet.

The Internet is certain to play an increasingly significant role in how business is done and the management of brands. Those interested in building and maintaining strong brands need to understand and exploit the Internet's power, integrating it with offline efforts.

B2B e-commerce Order Flow

The order flow and site functionality for B2B e-commerce sites can be broken down into seven main steps - issuing a tender, distributing tenders to specific companies/lists, receiving bids, negotiating contracts, issuing and tracking contracts, recording fulfillment of contracts, paying for services/goods via credit card / EFT. The following narrative describes the process and assumes that all parties are already members of the B2B system.

A registered purchaser enters the site and logs in

1. A site may use digital certificates as an additional method of verifying a user's identity.

The purchaser records the details of the goods/services they would like to purchase

1. Purchaser either creates a new tender or accesses an tender that has not yet been issued
2. Purchaser fills out all required information on the goods/services they wish to purchase
3. Purchaser proceeds to the issue tender function after the tender has been completed

The purchaser selects criteria as to which users should receive the tender

1. The purchaser may choose to issue the tender to all interested parties or to a selected list of companies that have been pre-screened.

System sends notification via email to appropriate suppliers that a new tender is available

1. Through either the secure email system or through regular email (without details), the system sends tender information to the appropriate suppliers.
2. Email may include attached tender document or may just provide a secure link to the tender location on the B2B site.

Notified suppliers review new tenders

1. This process may take place online or through a review of the attached formatted tender documents.

Interested suppliers issue a bid for the tender

1. Supplier login into the B2B site and record the details of their bid.

2. System may allow suppliers to attach a bid document to the tender or email it securely to the prospective purchaser.
3. System may prevent suppliers from bidding on a tender after the specified close date, or may just rely on a manual process by the purchasers.

System notifies the purchaser of a tender close

1. Notification could be through email or a daily report of closed tenders.
2. System will provide a list of suppliers who submitted a bid before the tender close date.

Purchaser reviews bids for tender

1. This process may take place online or through a review of attached bids.
2. Certain aspects of bids may be presented to the purchaser through the B2B site in a form that allows for easy comparison.
3. A B2B site could include weighting of criteria and provide automatic bid ranking based on the purchaser defined criteria for the specific tender.

If required, the purchaser contacts supplier(s) to clarify bids

1. The contact could be through secure email or telephone/fax.
2. More sophisticated systems will provide online discussion rooms for one-on-one and group tender clarification meetings (real time).
3. As technology improves, some B2B sites may offer video conferencing options for the clarification process.

Purchaser approves a bid

1. Bid is marked as approved and stamped with a digital certificate.

System notifies suppliers of success or failure of bids

1. Successful suppler will be notified of how and when to contact the purchaser to clarify any additional details.
2. Suppliers for unsuccessful bids are notified and possibly given reasons that their bid was not chosen.
3. Sophisticated systems may provide a ranking system for second and third bid choices.

Successful bid holder acknowledges approval and negotiates delivery specifics

1. Acknowledgement is recorded in the system and marked with the supplier's digital signature.
2. Supplier provides any details for delivery and payment details as required by system/purchaser.

Supplier arranges for deliver of goods/services

1. Supplier provides goods/services through standard channels.
2. Advanced systems for services may provide tracking systems for time and effort contracts and well as reporting for purchaser to track progress.
3. Goods systems may provide links to shipping systems so that supplier/purchaser can track shipments

Delivering party marks with digital signature that the goods/services have been filled

1. Done online through B2B system.

2. Delivery system may provide wireless or web-based integration so that signature for receipt of delivery is captured by B2B system directly.

Receiving party marks with digital signature that the goods/services have been filled

1. Allows purchaser opportunity to officially indicate that goods/services were received in good order.
2. May result from email notification or a standardized timed process (weekly/monthly).

System transfers appropriate funds from purchasers account to sellers account via credit card transaction or bank to bank transfer via EFT

1. After approval from the purchaser, B2B system securely connects to a bank and transfers money from the purchaser's account to supplier's account.
2. System records success of EFT payment or any errors reported (NSF etc.).
3. Parties are notified of completed transaction and contract is stored for reference.

Benefits of e-commerce Solutions

E-commerce solutions have the potential to provide adopters with a set of benefits over and above the ability to sell there products. These benefits can in some cases be the main reasons for choosing an e-commerce solution over or in conjunction with a traditional commerce solution. Some benefits of e-commerce apply to both B2C and B2B solutions, while some apply only to one. Below, the various potential benefits are examined.

1. *Global Reach*: Unlike traditional commerce solutions in which the selling or tendering process is likely limited to the immediate business area or in areas where branch offices are present, e-commerce allows a company to have a branch office everywhere in the world. The result of a good e-commerce solution is that customers from around the world have the opportunity to see and purchase goods or respond to tenders.

2. *Lower Staffing Costs*: e-commerce solutions hold the promise of reducing the staff costs needed to make a sale or sign a contract. As a result of having the selling and tender process online, the amount of interaction with staff is minimized. A well designed e-commerce site will allow users to resolve most issues without the need for intervention by staff.

3. *Integrated Payments with Banking and Accounting*: e-commerce solutions often have either credit card billing, or banking support for electronic funds transfer. As a result, the collection of monies owed can be automated, reducing the need for collections and bounced cheques. Advanced systems may even provide for robust support for accounting systems, reducing the overall book keeping required to successfully run a business.

4. *Increased Response Times*: In traditional commerce, sales and tenders often take a long time to move from the "just looking" to the buying stage. In e-commerce, the interaction with the system takes place in almost real time and therefore allows the customer or bidder to respond more quickly and reduces the lag time between discussion and purchase.

5. *Decreased Cost to Implement*: While technology is often quite expensive, a good e-commerce solution will not only provide a cost effective sales mechanism, but also an accounting, fulfillment and reporting solution that normally requires a significant IT expenditure in traditional commerce activities. As a result of this offset, and because of the gradual reduction in costs as better e-commerce tools develop, the e-commerce solution is often very cost effective to implement when compared to traditional commerce IT requirements.

Costs of e-commerce Solutions

While e-commerce solutions have the potential to provide adopters with a set of benefits over and above the ability to sell there products, there also exists some costs which must be weighed against these benefits when considering and e-commerce solution. Some costs of e-commerce apply to both B2C and B2B solutions, while others are specific to only one type. Below, the various potential costs are examined.

1. *Marketing Costs*: In traditional commerce solutions, the marketing costs are directly targeted to one tightly focused market. However, in e-commerce solutions, world wide focus can often result in a marketing effort that is too diverse and not keyed to the appropriate market segment. Just because you can sell goods to the entire world does not mean you should!

2. *Business Process Changes*: One major area in which most companies fail to accurately realize the costs of moving to an e-commerce solution is in the staff time

and energy needed to revamp the business process used to handle e-commerce transactions. Too many companies assume their existing process will be able to handle efficiently the e-commerce business. This assumption often results in substandard e-commerce solutions or in a situation where all the potential benefits are lost.

3. *Shipping Versus Staffing*: A major area of per unit cost for e-commerce solutions is that of the shipping of goods to the customer. Unlike bulk shipping of goods from a warehouse to a store, the shipping of e-commerce orders can be staff time and cost intensive. These costs can eat up all the potential savings in sales staff. In a highly competitive hard goods market, these costs can result in losses for a company looking to establish market position (look at any number of big name B2C companies for an example of this problem).

4. *Loss of Contact Customers*: As a result of the impersonal nature of the Internet, the shopping experience can be one where the customer does not feel they have received sufficient personal attention. Hard to hold someone's hand in cyberspace.

5. *Development and Setup / Maintenance Costs and Learning Curve*: While e-commerce solutions are getting more sophisticated and cost effective, the reality is that a custom solution is still often more expensive than most companies realize up front. In fact, the main problem can be that the appropriate solution is not understood by the company and as a result they get an e-commerce solution that is not necessarily appropriate for their goals.

6. *Relies on Customers and Suppliers Being Online*: The final limitation that e-commerce solutions have is one most people ignore - the customers and suppliers must be online with a connection fast enough and secure enough to effectively shop or respond to tenders. The result could be a limiting of the market potential in the short term. However, with the rate of growth of Internet use in the consumer and business markets over the past five years, it looks as if this limit may be removed sooner rather than later.

   The process of evaluating whether or not e-commerce is a cost effective decision for any particular business depends on what that business is trying to accomplish. In other words, what systems they already have in place, what their market is and what level of technical and business knowledge they already posses. While it would be a poor decision to ignore the business potential of e-commerce, it would be just as poor to assume that merely getting online will solve your business problems.

e-commerce Site Types and Techniques

The first type of e-commerce solution to discuss is the extension of an existing physical retailer. This e-commerce solution is the most familiar to consumers, as everything from well established brand stores to the local corner store are getting online. The process of extending a physical store to have an e-commerce portion can provide additional positive sales to an existing store, but carries with it additional issues, including some that pure e-commerce solutions may not have to face. These concerns include: integration with legacy technology, integration with business legacies, and added competition from pure e-commerce solutions.

First of all, the traditional stores may already have an inventory and a distribution system. These legacy systems (i.e., the systems that existed before the e-commerce solution) can require custom solutions for integration with the new e-commerce technologies. Often these solutions can be difficult, and as a result a good number of existing stores have taken the approach of making the e-commerce solutions act as separate online entities.

The idea is that these online stores will be better able to compete with other e-commerce stores without having the difficulties or burdens of the existing physical stores. This solution to the technological legacies can result in conflicts with the existing business systems.

As a result of or in addition to the technical legacies, physical stores that extend to have an e-commerce presence can also run into a number of business legacies. The most profound issue can be that the e-commerce site will often be viewed as a competitor to the existing stores within a chain. If not managed properly, this issue can be an area of contention, given that an e-commerce store has a potentially infinite territory. In addition to territory overlap, e-commerce stores may also carry different pricing than the physical stores. As a result, customers can come to expect e-commerce stores to be tied to their local physical store and be able to make returns and pick up purchases. Failure to accommodate this may result in a situation in which the customer is poorly serviced and the brand as a whole suffers.

Finally, traditional stores that attempt to use the e-commerce solution as an extension of their physical store are faced with a serious challenge from new pure e-commerce competitors. These new players in the market have yet to prove themselves as viable business units, but during this process of discovery physical stores can be faced with additional price and supply pressures that have not previously been experienced.

Pure e-commerce Solution

A pure e-commerce solution is one in which the web based store is the only commerce solution for that particular company. This area of e-commerce solutions brings some of the most recognizable names to our computer screens (GaltBooks, eToys) with the key being that the e-commerce solution for these stores are the only solution used; that is that they have no physical stores.

Still, this type of e-commerce solution has a number of difficulties that are in some ways trade-offs from the difficulties experienced by existing stores: no infrastructure to build on, zero brand recognition, and low retention of customers.

Unlike extensions to physical stores, pure e-commerce solutions do not have any existing infrastructure to build upon. While in some cases this can be easier to implement as a result of not having to deal with integration, this also means that the pure e-commerce solutions cannot leverage any of that infrastructure. As a result, pure e-commerce solutions are often faced with greater upfront development / software costs, or they decide to manually handle some functions. While the manual functionality works for a smaller site, at a certain point this solution is not cost effective as volume rises.

The second area in which pure e-commerce solutions have challenges is that of establishing brand recognition. This problem represents the fact that pure e-commerce solutions need (or at least think they need) to spend large amounts of capital to establish a brand name.

With traditional retail solutions, the brand names have already been established and can be leveraged online. The question that remains is whether or not the pure e-commerce strategy will result in long run sustainable brand recognition, or whether they will expire before reaching critical mass.

Related to the brand recognition issue is that of customer loyalty. As the ballooning sales and marketing costs result in higher costs per customer for pure e-commerce solutions, the entire industry is beginning to question whether the current approach to this type of e-commerce solution is sustainable.

According to recent studies, it costs the average e-commerce site $82 to attach one customer of which they keep 27 percent, in comparison to $12 per customer with 34 percent retention rate for traditional retail (Boston Consulting Group). Not surprising, at this rate of capital burn, a number of pure e-commerce solutions in recent months are rethinking their solution in light of declining war chests and potential bankruptcy fallout in the industry.

Auctions Sites

The final type of e-commerce solution that has come online to date is that of an auction site. In this solution, the site acts as a broker for the various parties, be they business or consumers. This area of e-commerce solution takes a different approach in that they make available their technology to all parties for a fee. Rather than being a store and selling goods, the e-commerce solution is selling services. While there exists some promise to this type of e-commerce solution, there still exists a number of difficulties for this type: market saturation with competition, similar high costs of brand awareness, and the need for strategic alliances to provide a consistently desirable flow of goods.

As with pure e-commerce solutions, auction sites face the potential problem that e-commerce competition has the tendency to sprout up over-night. The result is that this area is quickly becoming saturated with all purpose and special purpose auction sites. The potential difficulty with this can be the fragmentation of this type of approach with users being unsure of who to use (i.e., what site will get me the highest price or offer the best selection). This problem leads directly into the same problem as pure e-commerce sites: brand awareness costs.

As with pure e-commerce solutions, auction sites often have a high cost for developing brand awareness. The result can often be that large sums of money are also spent promoting the auction site. Since the business offers a low per unit margin, these sites rely on traffic from sellers and buyers. As the market shakes out, it is likely that the numerous sites will under go consolidation with the better positioned sites winning. And the positioning that matters is ...?

In a phase the key to auction site success comes from strategic alliances. The most success sites will have alliances with the major players in the suppliers of goods. This will often mean that auctions sites will take on the position as acting as the re-seller for larger players in specific industries. A prime example of this can be seen in the airline industries, where a number of carriers release unsold inventory to auction sites for resale. For the suppliers of goods that go stale rapidly, the solution allows them to recoup some of the value of these goods prior to their expiry. While all types of e-commerce solutions have potential advantages, they all also have difficulties that need to be overcome in order to be successful. In most cases, these difficulties are not truly technical difficulties, but rather business issues that can be resolved through clear leadership and innovative strategies. As with any technology, the Internet e-commerce solutions simply provide options for companies, with the good companies being distinguished by the path they choose.

E-commerce Build Versus Buy Decisions

While the decision to implement an e-commerce solution can be based on a high level strategic decision, the actual method of implementation can vary. The implementation choices can be broken down into two basic approaches: build versus buy. The areas of influence that can influence this decision are as with any software project: functionality requirements, scalability desires, resource allocations, and standard/brand requirements. Once all of these areas have been reviewed, the options for buying and building will be compared and a decision made.

Functionality

Generally the most critical factor in the decision as to whether to build or buy an e-commerce solution is the functionality. As with any software project, the first step in coming to a decision should be the determination of the software requirements and the categorization of the requirements in to three categories: must have, nice to have, and frills. For e-commerce sites (depending on the type), the requirements will generally be chosen from the following:

— shopping cart
— order data collection
— customer data collection
— product data collection
— email
— shipping integration
— tax handling
— searching and browsing
— credit card validation
— electronic funds payments
— fullfilment
— reporting
— tender and bid management
— contract management
— online communications
— security

As a general rule of thumb, a solution that provides for all must have requirements and 80 percent of the other requirements is considered a good fit to the functionality. If functionality is critical and specific, then an e-commerce solution will likely lean towards a build solution due to the flexibility offered in this approach. Of course, functionality needed today is not the only concern in choosing between building and buying. In addition, the future requirements or scalability/robustness of the system needs to be considered.

Scalability

While functionality determines what an e-commerce site will do, scalability determines the ability of the system to handle increases in the amount of use as well as the ability to modify/maintain the system over the course of time. The scalability factor is a basic determination as to how much growth and change is anticipated by project for the life of the project. The critical issues for scalability in terms of usage are short term growth/peaks in usage as well as long term growth. A particular solution must be robust enough to provide for short term spikes in usage. A typical example of this would be a cyclical solution such as an online toy store.

Since toys are particularly popular around Christmas, these types of solutions must be able to handle the expected increase in the Christmas seasons. In the 1999 Christmas season, a number of online toy stores experienced failures in handling the two to three times increase in traffic. The result was late gifts and unhappy customers. In terms of long term growth, e-commerce sites must estimate the level of growth that a site will experience over the medium to long term, which in Internet terms is usually the 1-3 year timeframe. Since e-commerce growth is often 100-200 percent a year (at this stage), the ability to meet growth can be very critical.

In addition to growth, e-commerce solutions will need to be evaluated in terms of future functionality and maintainability. In this area, scalability will include the ability for a site owner to maintain and change the site over the course of time. This factor will reflect the long term expectations for the site. The e-commerce solution will need to be evaluated in terms of the need to change and upgrade the site functionality over time. If the site planners feel that the functionality will be constant for the medium to long term then scalability will not be a major issue in the build versus buy decision. However, if the site will change rapidly, then the scalability issue will often push towards a build solution as it will generally provide a greater level of control and flexibility.

Resources

In addition to the scalability, an e-commerce solution will need to be evaluated in terms of the resources an organization has to dedicate to the project. The resources relevant to the discussion of build versus buy are money and in house technical expertise. In terms of costs for e-commerce solutions, the general rule should be that to buy an equivalently functional solution should be less expensive than a custom built solution. While this is not always the case, the reason for it is that a bought solution will be generally less flexible and will have the costs of development spread over multiple clients. In addition, custom solutions will often have less certain costs, as estimates are based on the requirements which can (and often do) change over time. As a result, e-commerce solutions that are particularly sensitive to costs or have fixed budgets should probably seriously consider the buy options.

In addition to the resources need to build or buy a solution, a company must consider the resources needed to maintain and administer the technology. Since both built and bought solutions will have these needs, the real question here will be whether or not a particular build or buy solution is based on technology that company has internal support for or can acquire externally. Since the buy options are generally limited in the technological choices, internal resources may eliminate some particular solutions as options. The build option has infinite flexibility, and while the actual technology choices will be affected, the choice to build will not.

Standards and Brands

The final area that needs to be considered in the e-commerce build versus buy decision is that of technological standards support and brands. These areas will often add another dimension of constraints to the solution chosen, and in some ways may be competing concepts.

Standards support by a particular solution will help to ensure that the solution is not tied directly to one vendor, or that the solution will inter-operate with other standardized approaches. Areas of standardization can include development language, data transmission, HTML level (for browser compatibility) and transaction processing. Since both built and bought solutions can support a variety of standards, this factor will generally only be used to eliminate specific build / buy options.

In addition to comparing build / buy options for standards support, organizations may also have a marketing or strategic partnership need to choose a solution that utilizes a particular brand of technology. While the top brands in each area of technology can have distinct advantages in terms of support and public perception, the technological impact may be not be as large.

As a result, the real issue is whether or not a particular build / buy decision supports the business choice of technology brand. If the technology brand issue is not important, then this fact need not be included in the build versus buy decision.

Lately there has been a real buzz about Application Service Providers (ASPs). This concept provides a client with a solution that is provided standard by the vendor and hosted and maintained by the vendor. The e-commerce version of this solution is paid for though monthly fees and/or per unit fees. While some people may view this as a third possible option, in reality the rental option is really not a lot different then the buy option. The main difference will be in the upfront costs level (lower) versus the monthly costs (higher). Still for a cost sensitive e-commerce solution this route may change the build versus buy decision.

6

Advertising on Internet

Online classifieds might not be the most glamorous segment of Internet advertising, but the sector is poised to be one of the engines of growth in a rebounding market, according to a new study by Jupiter Media Metrix. According to the New York-based researcher, spending on online classified advertising grew 38 percent from 2001, rising to $1.2 billion this year. By 2007, that figure will almost double to $2.3 billion — making it the Web ad industry's fastest-growing segment.

Jupiter attributes much of this growth to marketers' increasing shift of offline ad dollars to the Internet — as illustrated by the 15 percent drop in traditional classified spending from 2001 to 2002. "Although 2001 was a transitional year for online advertising, the fundamental value remains clear," said Jupiter Research Senior Analyst Marissa Gluck. "Online advertising is a strong impetus of consumer action — including increasing traffic and sales, inspiring loyalty and promoting referrals." Overall, Jupiter predicts that the U.S. online ad market will to grow from $6.2 billion in 2002 to $15.9

billion in 2007, a compound annual growth rate of 21 percent. In 2007, online ad spending will represent about 7 percent of total U.S. ad spending, up significantly from the approximately 2 percent market share it currently enjoys.

While Jupiter also expects average impression-based ad prices will drop between 2001 and 2002 — from $2.60 to $2.50 per thousand impressions — analysts believe media consolidation and larger-format ads will drive prices back up. F

As with most attempts to calculate and predict industry-wide revenue, Jupiter's figures doesn't match other researchers' findings. In their most recent findings, PricewaterhouseCoopers and the Interactive Advertising Bureau (IAB), for example, found that classified ads grew from 4 percent of the industry's 2000 revenue ($184 million) to 10 percent (or $820 million) of 2001 spending.

Contributing to the rise in Internet classified advertising is the proliferation of online real estate listings. Research from Borrell Associates indicates that some realtors have begun shifting home listings away from local print media to their own Web sites, where they hope to find a better return on investment.

The study, based on in-depth interviews with agents, brokers and multiple listing service (MLS) executives across the U.S., illustrates a growing population that has shifted from newspaper readership to the Web. Realtors spend approximately $3.5 billion per year on real estate advertising in newspapers, representing 5.8 percent of total newspaper revenues, and an additional $3 billion is annually budgeted for free-distribution rack publications. The rising cost of newspaper classified advertising, compounded by a poor return on investment, sets up the perfect opportunity for a move to the Web by realtors.

Borrell anticipates that newspapers will still play a significant role in the real estate industry, where they are strongly positioned to provide more dynamic, cross-media packages that give realtors better lead generation and increased interactive functionality. But first, newspapers will need to step up to the plate and recognize that the Internet has revolutionized the real estate market.

The challenging issue of online ad impression measurement, which has been labeled as the top priority of the Interactive Advertising Bureau (IAB), has been addressed by guidelines developed by an IAB-lead industry consortium of organizations and companies. With the participation of the Advertising Research Foundation (ARF), ABC Interactive (ABCi), and the Media Rating Council (MRC), and supported by the American Association of Advertising Agencies (AAAA) and the Association of National Advertisers (ANA), the IAB is introducing these voluntary guidelines in order to make interactive advertising easier to buy.

Based on an extensive six-month study conducted by PricewaterhouseCoopers, the guidelines, which identify and define five key metrics in the measurement process - ad impressions, clicks, visits, "unique" measurements (browsers, visitors and users), and page impressions - point to site-side data disclosure as being integral to accurate measurement and reporting of interactive advertising data.

Based on the independently conducted PwC study, which included the active participation of AOL, Atlas

DMT, CNET Networks, Inc., Walt Disney Internet Group, DoubleClick, Forbes.com, MSN, New York Times Digital, Terra Lycos and Yahoo!, the Media Rating Council (MRC) lead the industry committee in the creation of the actual guidelines. The study's primary objectives were to:

1) review the current measurement criteria and practices used by the sell-side participants for online advertising and audience measurement reporting;

2) determine and report the comparability of existing metrics used by the industry; and

3) propose a common set of industry definitions and guidelines for data analysis and reporting.

The cooperation of the participants —the IAB, the participating media companies, PwC, the ARF, ABCi and the MRC -- has made this document very strong. The discipline driven by strong filtration procedures, the standardization of the measurement metrics, disclosure and auditing specifics will improve the consistency and accuracy of Internet site and ad-server measurements, providing the enhanced confidence advertisers and agencies need.

For the past five years ANA members have been surveyed regarding their Internet advertising activity and lack of reliable and accurate measurement information consistently rank in the top three reasons why ANA member companies do not purchase more interactive advertising.

In compiling their report, all of the participating organizations supplied information to Price-waterhouseCoopers on their measurement criteria and practices and cooperated in interviews and testing. PwC's procedures included interviews with employees, reviews of policies, definitions and procedures, execution of scripted testing used to assess the collection and reporting systems and analyses of results for differences and for the purpose of suggesting consistent definitions.

"As online advertising becomes an integral part of mainstream advertisers' media mix, advertisers are demanding more accountability," said Tom Hyland, Partner and Chair of PricewaterhouseCoopers New Media practice. "At the same time, the process, systems and data metrics supporting online advertising are becoming more complex. These guidelines go a long way in helping make online advertising an easier buy for advertisers and agencies. PricewaterhouseCoopers is proud to play an integral role in this comprehensive industry effort."

"These voluntary guidelines for ad campaign measurement and audits are a milestone in the growth of the interactive advertising industry as they are focused on creating a consistency among all parties to the process," said IAB President & CEO, Greg Stuart. "These guidelines, backed up by the master list of spiders and robots that ABCi has created, and the glossary of terms which the IAB issued several months ago are expected to eliminate between fifty and seventy per cent of the discrepancies that now exist. These guidelines provide benchmarks from which our industry can now be effectively audited."

Online Ad Banners

The majority of all online ad banners have short life spans, running on average three weeks or less, according to a new report released by AdRelevance, a division of

Media Metrix. With few advertisers running large online campaigns, an overwhelming majority of advertisers have less than a 0.01 percent share of all online advertising impressions..

Key findings from the latest AdRelevance Intelligence Report, which analyzes standard 468x60 banner ad campaigns on the top 500 Web sites between July 1999 and June 2000, include:

Although most banner ads run for three or fewer weeks, the average banner runs for five and a half weeks. The automotive industry schedules online ads to run the longest, an average of 7.8 weeks. This is almost twice as long as the average banner duration for a hardware and electronics ad, which typically lasts 4.1 weeks. The consumer goods industry embraces the most targeted ad approaches, with only 40 percent of online impressions appearing on broad reach sites like portals, search engines and community destinations. At the other end of the spectrum, Web media, financial services and travel advertisers appear to be targeting the least, running an overwhelming majority of ad impressions on broad reach sites.

While the average campaign in the second quarter weighed in at 7,265,000 impressions, more than half of all advertisers ran campaigns with less than 44,000 impressions. A campaign this small would only garner a 0.0003 percent share of voice on a major portal like Yahoo!.

Automotive industry runs banner ads almost twice as long as hardware and electronics advertisers Broad reach more popular than targeted approach for recent online campaigns. "While most advertisers are running relatively short campaigns, shorter campaigns are not necessarily better campaigns," said Charlie Buchwalter, vice president of media research for the AdRelevance division of Media Metrix. "

Although shorter campaigns may concentrate banner impressions, thereby increasing the share of voice and share of market for an advertiser, only longer campaigns can bring about a change in consumer attitudes and behavior. The latest AdRelevance findings suggest that automotive, financial services and travel advertisers are out to change behavior because they are running banners the longest, when compared to other industries."

The AdRelevance Intelligence Report analyzes ad impression distribution strategies for campaigns running four, eight and 12 weeks - revealing that banner impressions, on average, are heavier in the beginning of four and 12 week campaigns. On the other hand, campaigns running eight weeks tend to feature higher impression levels in the middle. Impressions for the average banner in an eight week campaign peaked in the fifth week.

"There is no golden rule when it comes to campaign continuity, but it appears that advertisers are adopting two weighting approaches - either front-loading for shorter campaigns or pulsing for longer campaigns," Buchwalter said. "The conclusions from this AdRelevance Intelligence Report support the fact that the online advertising market is still in its infancy, and has a way to go before analysts can accurately determine what constitutes an effective and successful online ad campaign. We'll know things are changing when more companies commit to larger, longer and more targeted online campaigns."

According to a New eAdvertising Report: U.S. Web Ad Spending Will Increase To $6 Billion By Year End 2000

— U.S. Web Ad Spending Will Increase To $6 Billion By Year End From $3.6 Billion In 1999

— The Online Market Will Rise To $21 Billion by 2004

— Large Percentage Growth Online Will Still Only Represent 4.7% of Total Ad Media Spending by 2003

U.S. web advertising spending more than doubled in 1999 to 3.6 billion, up from 1.7 billion in 1998. This same trend will follow through to year-end 2000 when advertising spending will increase by 69% to reach a high of $6 billion, according to eMarketer's eAdvertising Report. The report also reveals that the online market will rise to $21 billion by 2004, 3.5 times its size this year.

The report, by New York-based eMarketer, also reveals that active Latin American internet users in the region will equal 5% of the 372 million users worldwide by 2003. The report also reveals that although these numbers indicate that the Latin American user base may be big enough to create a lucrative market, it will not challenge the North American or European regions for a very long time. "My conclusion from these numbers is that this thing is really booming," said the report's author, Senior Analyst David Halprin. "Internet advertising really is something that potentially will be more effective advertising than anything the world has ever known."

Halprin also adds that many research analysts have upwardly revised their ad revenue projections. According to the eAdvertising Report, composite 1999 online and ad revenue projections from about 15 researchers were $2.6

billion in January 1999, $3.1 billion in December 1999 and $3.6 billion in April 2000.

Despite tremendous growth of online advertising over the past two years, the eAdvertising report indicates that the advancements will slow as the as the industry stabilizes and future trends become more established.

Growth in on-line advertising will be affected by the following trends:

— Advertisers and their agencies will continue to tinker with critical issues such as measurement, standards, ROI and privacy

— Web advertising will be embraced by large consumer marketing companies and attain a more strategic position within corporate marketing budgets

— Online advertisers will continue their struggle to achieve a measurable return on investment

Key Findings of eAdvertising Report:

— The US dominance of online ad spending, like user penetration rates and e-commerce development, is slipping. Europe is the next frontier, with 9% of global web expenditures in 1999 and rising to 18% by 2004

— The banner ad is still the standard advertising form on the web, accounting for 50% of all online dollars placed in 1999. By the end of 2003 banners will decline to 41% of web ad sales, with strategic sponsorships taking 30%.

— By year-end 1999, the top 10 publisher sites accounted for 74% of ad dollars earned, and by year-end 2000 this figure will reach 76%. Currently, the top 50 web publishers generate 95% of all web revenues.

— General portal sites will capture only 34% of web advertising dollars by 2004

— Savvy web advertisers will exploit new techniques and technologies to drive direct response and achieve ROI.

The US Federal Trade Commission (FTC) Act allows the FTC to act in the interest of all consumers to prevent deceptive and unfair acts or practices. In interpreting Section 5 of the Act, the Commission has determined that a representation, omission or practice is deceptive if it is likely to:

— mislead consumers and

— affect consumers' behavior or decisions about the product or service.

In addition, an act or practice is unfair if the injury it causes, or is likely to cause, is:

— substantial

— not outweighed by other benefits and

— not reasonably avoidable.

The FTC Act prohibits unfair or deceptive advertising in any medium. That is, advertising must tell the truth and not mislead consumers. A claim can be misleading if relevant information is left out or if the claim implies something that's not true. For example, a lease advertisement for an automobile that promotes "$0 Down" may be misleading if significant and undisclosed charges are due at lease signing.

In addition, claims must be substantiated, especially when they concern health, safety, or performance. The type of evidence may depend on the product, the claims, and what experts believe necessary. If your ad specifies a certain level of support for a claim - "tests show X" - you must have at least that level of support.

Sellers are responsible for claims they make about their products and services. Third parties - such as advertising agencies or website designers and catalog marketers - also may be liable for making or disseminating deceptive representations if they participate in the preparation or distribution of the advertising, or know about the deceptive claims.

— Advertising agencies or website designers are responsible for reviewing the information used to substantiate ad claims. They may not simply rely on an advertiser's assurance that the claims are substantiated. In determining whether an ad agency should be held liable, the FTC looks at the extent of the agency's participation in the preparation of the challenged ad, and whether the agency knew or should have known that the ad included false or deceptive claims.

— To protect themselves, catalog marketers should ask for material to back up claims rather than repeat what the manufacturer says about the product. If the manufacturer doesn't come forward with proof or turns over proof that looks questionable, the catalog marketer should see a yellow "caution light" and proceed appropriately, especially when it comes to extravagant performance claims, health or weight loss promises, or earnings guarantees. In writing ad copy, catalogers should stick to claims that can be supported. Most important, catalog marketers should trust their instincts when a product sounds too good to be true.

Other points to consider:

— Disclaimers and disclosures must be clear and conspicuous. That is, consumers must be able to notice, read or hear, and understand the information. Still, a disclaimer or disclosure alone usually is not enough to remedy a false or deceptive claim.

— Demonstrations must show how the product will perform under normal use.

— Refunds must be made to dissatisfied consumers - if you promised to make them.

— Advertising directed to children raises special issues. That's because children may have greater difficulty evaluating advertising claims and understanding the nature of the information you provide. Sellers should take special care not to misrepresent a product or its performance when advertising to children. The Children's Advertising Review Unit (CARU) of the Council of Better Business Bureaus has published specific guidelines for children's advertising that you may find helpful.

Information About Online Advertising, an FTC staff paper, provides additional information for online advertisers. The paper discusses the factors used to evaluate the clarity and conspicuousness of required disclosures in online ads. It also discusses how certain FTC rules and guides that use terms like "writing" or "printed" apply to Internet activities and how technologies such as email may be used to comply with certain rules and guides.

7

Consumer Privacy on Internet

The growth of e-commerce has created threats to consumers' privacy on an unprecedented scale. Details about a user's private life are now an open book for those who wish to track down such information, yet consumers often do not know that every time they use the internet, they leave behind a detailed trail of personal information. Financial and personal information is stolen every day and used fraudulently to purchase goods and get credit.

Many sensitive documents, such as financial and medical records that were previously stored in separate databases, can now be placed online, frequently without consumer consent or adequate privacy protection. Consumers International's research reveals that internet sites selling products and services to consumers in the United States and Europe fall woefully short of international standards on data protection. Most sites collect personal information but fail to tell consumers how that data will be used, how security is maintained, and what rights consumers have over their own information.

Despite tight European Union (EU) legislation, sites within the EU are no better at providing decent information to their customers than sites based in the US. Indeed some of the best privacy policies are to be found on US sites. Concerns over confidentiality and security rank highly amongst reasons why consumers are reluctant to buy goods and services online.

Unless policy makers and companies address issues of data protection, these concerns will continue to be well-justified, and electronic commerce may suffer as a result. The objective of this research project was to find out how much information is collected from consumers when using the internet – whether for browsing, personal research or shopping – and to see how many sites take steps to protect the privacy of this information.

By assessing more than 750 sites, Consumers International aimed to establish whether there was a significant difference in approach among internet sites based in the European Union and the United States. This chapter starts by providing some general background to the issues surrounding electronic commerce and privacy.

Despite the fact that the majority of the sites collected personal information from the user, only a tiny minority provided a privacy policy that gave users meaningful information about how that data would be used. Sites both in the US and EU fall woefully short of the standards set by international guidelines on data protection. The majority of sites ignore even the most basic principles of fair information use, such as telling consumers how their data will be used; how it can be accessed; what choices the consumer has about its use; and how security of that data is maintained. This widespread neglect of good privacy practice is made all the more worrying in the electronic commerce medium, where technologies for collection and use of data are developing so rapidly. Despite tight EU legislation in this area, researchers did not find that sites based in the EU gave better information or a higher degree of choice to their users than sites based in the US. Indeed, US-based sites tended to set the standard for decent privacy policies.

As US consumers do not have legal protection in this area, companies have to make more effort to reassure their users that their privacy will be protected. EU consumers are not only protected by legislation, but also have a data protection commissioner in each country looking out for their rights, and have a right to redress if the law is breached. However, in practice, EU sites do no better than US ones at keeping their users informed. Indeed it appears that many EU sites are failing to comply with EU rules that state that the consumer must be given the right to opt out if their data is to be used for direct marketing purposes.

The following section provides a summary of the most important findings of the website assessment. A fuller account of these findings and the underlying data is given in pages 22 to 27.

- Just over two thirds of the sites assessed (67%) collected some sort of personal information about the visitor during the process of using the site.
- Almost all sites that collected information asked for details that made it easy to identify and contact that person. Name, email name, postal address information and phone number were the most common type of information requested. The exception to this was news and information-type sites

that tended to just ask visitors where they live in order to provide local news or weather.

- Most sites let the visitor visit and browse without overtly collecting information from them, but most encourage users to give information in order to use the site fully, for example by "personalising" the site, or signing up for membership. This enables the user to receive information that may be relevant to his or her life (for example local news and weather or a newsletter), but also provides an opportunity for the site to collect plenty of data about the consumer.
- Fifty-eight percent of the sites that collected. Research findings: overall verdict information had a privacy policy. Of sites that collected personal information from their users, *health* sites were the least likely to have a privacy policy. *Most popular* sites within the US were the most likely to have a privacy policy. *Most popular* sites based in the EU, and US-based *financial* sites, also performed well.
- Privacy policies, however, were not always easily accessible. Only a third (32.5%) of sites that collected information and had a privacy policy alerted visitors to that privacy policy at the point where the information was collected. US-based *most popular* sites performed best, with 62.5% signposting their privacy policy at the point where information was collected. Sites should also signpost their privacy policies from their home page. Researchers found that just over a third of sites (39%) signposted their privacy policy from their home page. US-based sites were much more likely to do this than EU-based ones. 97.5% of US-based *most popular* sites signposted privacy policies from their home page.

- The vast majority of sites gave customers no choice about being on the site's own mailing list, having the customer's name passed on to affiliates, or to third parties. US *most popular* sites were most likely to give users a choice, despite the existence of legislation that obliges EU-based sites to provide consumers with a choice.
- Having a document called a privacy policy doesn't count for much unless it provides adequate information for the consumer. Very few of the privacy policies Consumers International assessed contained more than the bare minimum of information, and only a minority gave important information about the control consumers can have over their own data.
- However comprehensive a privacy policy is, it is worthless if the company fails to abide by it. Consumers International has found that some companies do breach their own policies. Therefore effective enforcement and a right to redress for consumers are vital.

Fair Information Principles

Over the past three decades, countries have established a set of principles for data protection. These are commonly known as "fair information principles", or FIPS. The US Department of Health, Education and Welfare first proposed the principles in 1974 and they were adopted into law in numerous countries. In 1981, the Organisation for Economic Cooperation and Development released extended guidelines based on the FIPS and the Council of Europe incorporated them into a treaty for the processing of personal information in computerised systems that have been widely adopted in Europe.

Despite the widespread acceptance of these practices, Consumers International's research shows that the majority of sites ignore even the most basic principles of fair information use, such as: giving consumers control over the collection and use of their information; giving them a right to access and correct that information; and ensuring security of their data.

Because so many companies ignore basic fair information principles, policy makers at the national and international level need to take urgent action to ensure that consumers are adequately protected. The following principles need to be incorporated into companies' internal practices and national governments' enforceable laws:

Collection of personal information

Information should only be collected if it is essential to the transaction. Any collection of nonessential information should be optional and clearly marked as such. Sensitive information (as defined in international agreements such as the COE Convention 108 and the EU Data Protection Directive) should not be collected about the consumer except in very limited circumstances.

Information must be obtained directly from the consumer unless the consumer gives his or her prior consent allowing the information to be collected from another source. The organisation should state the reason for collecting the information it has requested. Information should be collected by fair and lawful means. Sites should never collect personal data in a non-transparent manner – for example by using hidden mechanisms such as web-bugs and cookies – without obtaining the consent of the consumer first. Whenever surveys, competitions or other forms of interaction are used to collect data, the organisation must make it clear to consumers that the information is being collected and how it will be used.

Use and disclosure of personal information

Personal information should be used only for the purpose for which it was collected, unless the consumer has given prior consent, as required by law. Personal information should be kept only as long as necessary to fulfil that purpose. Sensitive personal information should not be used or disclosed without the prior consent of the user.

If the organisation offers any options regarding using or disclosing personal information – such as passing it on to another company – the information should be available online and the consumer should be able to respond online. The user should not be told to write to a separate address in order to limit the use of his or her data.

If an organisation dissolves, files for bankruptcy, is acquired by another organisation, or otherwise changes legal status, it should obtain prior permission from the consumer before transferring the information to the new organisation. If the consumer does not grant permission, the information should be deleted.

All the above obligations must apply equally to any third party which receives personal information about a consumer, as well as to the original organisation that collects the information.

Access

Sites should provide users with access to all information held about them. Users should also be provided with information on systems which affect their legal rights through automatic processing (where a computer programme is used to make decisions about people). Users should be able to obtain this access speedily, and free of charge.

Sites should use methods to verify that such requests by consumers for access to data are genuine – to avoid giving out personal details to an impostor – but should not use such requests as an opportunity to gather yet more data.

An individual must be able to challenge the accuracy and completeness of their data and have it amended as appropriate. Sites should explain clearly how users can correct or delete their data.

Security

Organisations have an obligation to take both administrative and technical measures to ensure that information is collected, stored and transmitted in a secure manner. The level of security should be appropriate to the sensitivity of the data collected.

Oversight and Compliance

An organisation should make specific information about

its policies and practices relating to the management of personal information readily available to individuals.

An organisation is responsible for personal information under its control and should designate an individual or individuals who are accountable for the organisation's compliance with its privacy principles.

An individual should be able to address a challenge concerning compliance with the privacy principles to the designated individual or individuals accountable for the organisation's compliance.

National governments should establish an independent oversight body to ensure compliance and provide for adequate sanctions for violations.

Redress

Consumers should have access to an independent redress mechanism that is cheap, quick and effective. Policymakers must give urgent consideration to the issue of redress in cross-border situations.

Privacy policies

All sites that collect information from users should provide a privacy policy that clearly states their policy towards that information.

The privacy policy should be signposted in a clear and prominent manner from the home page, and at every point within the site where personal information is collected. The privacy policy should be written in a clear and easy to understand manner.

The privacy policy should include:

- the identity of the company that owns and operates the site
- the kind of information collected
- why the data is stored and what it is used for
- who the data is shared with (including a list of affiliates), and what choices the user has about this
- how long the data is stored for
- how the security of that data is ensured
- how consumers can access, alter and delete their data
- how the site's policy might change in the future
- contact details for the person responsible for the privacy of data
- contact information for the pertinent oversight body

Consumer action

Consumers should consider the existence and content of a privacy policy before submitting personal data to a site. This is particularly important when shopping from a site based in another country.

If consumers are concerned about privacy of their data, they should not use sites that do not adequately protect their data. In addition, they should consider tactics such as using a number of email accounts, or using a service that allows for anonymous browsing of the internet. Consumers International have developed a practical tip sheet for consumers who want to protect their privacy online.

Children

Children and young people should not be encouraged to give information about themselves, their household or about any other persons. Giving information should not be made a condition of gaining access to the site. Children and young people should not be offered rewards (money, gifts or anything else of a monetary value) for giving information. Non-transparent methods of data collection (such as surveys and competitions) should never be used to collect information from children. None of these policy recommendations are particularly radical, or call for anything that should not currently be common practice for companies. Indeed, in most cases, all Consumers International is calling for is that companies abide by existing legislation and guidelines regarding privacy of personal data.

Internet and Privacy

The internet has dramatically changed the world. An estimated 377 million individuals globally are now online. They are using the net to read news, talk to friends, buy goods, listen to music and for countless other activities. A significant number of people are using the internet to buy goods and services. As diverse networks of computers, telephones, television, cable and satellite merge, most activities in the developed world will be connected to online technology. A Forrester research survey estimates that US business to consumer internet sales will reach US$108 billion by 2002. When asked about their worries regarding online shopping, consumers have ranked invasion of privacy as a top concern. An American Express survey of 11,000 consumers in 10 countries found that 79 percent cited privacy and security as a major concern in relation to online shopping. This fear is turning many consumers away from using electronic commerce because they are concerned about the potential abuse of their personal information by electronic commerce companies.

A survey by the US National Consumer League found that privacy was one of consumers' highest concerns. Fifty seven percent of the respondents said that they had not bought anything online in the last 12 months because they were worried that either their credit card number or their personal information would be abused. Other consumers reported that they provide false information to protect themselves. Forrester research estimates that electronic-commerce sales were reduced by $2.8 billion in 1999 because of privacy concerns.

While the technologies are developing at breakneck speed, the policies governing their use and the traditional protections that consumers have enjoyed for over a generation have lagged behind. In addition, new issues, such as defining jurisdiction and law in a world where transactions can easily occur between individuals in different countries and on different continents urgently need to be addressed. Some technology is emerging to provide protection for consumers but the scope is limited. Even more confusing for consumers is the fact that frequently, privacy-invasive technology that actually encourages capturing of data is misleadingly promoted as protecting privacy.

The research study included in this chapter was coordinated by Consumers International and carried out by the same global research team. Consumers@shopping: an international comparative study of electronic commerce, published by Consumers International in September 1999, examined what happened when consumers bought a range of products over the internet. The aim was to find out how easy it was to shop on the internet, to identify problem areas, and to pinpoint good and bad practice. The shopping for this project was carried out in late 1998 and early 1999, and involved purchasing items both at home and abroad. A range of problems was identified. These included companies that provided inadequate information to the consumer; sent goods that arrived late or did not turn up at all; and delayed refunds.

One primary area targeted for criticism in the 1999 report was the sites' approach to data protection and privacy. Whilst almost all sites demanded certain pieces of personal information, only one in five explained to the consumer what use was made of this information. Most customers would expect to provide a minimum amount of information when buying something over the internet, but consumers do not necessarily want that information collected unless it is essential to the transaction. In particular, consumers do not want the information used for any purpose unrelated to the specific purchase they currently are conducting. The findings of Consumers@shopping indicated a great deal of interest in the privacy aspect of electronic commerce, and demonstrated a clear need for more detailed research.

Privacy

Privacy is usually described as "the right to be left alone." It defines the relationship between an individual and society, including government, companies and other individuals. It is recognised as a fundamental human right in the Universal Declaration of Human Rights, adopted by the United Nations in 1948, and other international treaties.

The range of issues that fall under the name of privacy is quite broad. These include secret communications and papers, protection of home and family, and bodily integrity. In electronic commerce, the protection of privacy concerns the setting of rules and limits on the collection, handling, and use of personal information that is gathered by companies and other organisations as part of the interaction between a consumer and those companies. This is commonly referred to as "data protection". Interest in data protection began in the 1960s with the increased use of computers in society. The collection and use of personal information by powerful computer systems prompted demands for specific rules governing the collection and handling of personal information.

Electronic commerce raises new concerns about privacy because the scope and detail of personal information collected about consumers is far greater than is usually collected in the off-line world. The internet environment allows businesses to collect, analyse and use more information about customers, and with more ease and efficiency than ever before. The possibilities for storing, comparing, and linking information to build up a detailed picture of a customer's interests are huge. There have always been concerns over the way businesses use personal information, but the ease with which they can collect and manipulate that information on the internet makes the scale of the problem much larger. To add to the complexity of the situation, the internet has the potential for opening up markets – both for shopping and information-gathering – in other countries, which have widely diverse laws governing data protection.

There are important differences between how information is collected on customers who shop online versus those who shop the old-fashioned way – on the high street and in the malls. Two of the most important differences are that most online companies keep track of users' visits and purchases. Unlike most consumer transactions off-line, detailed information is collected about individuals' actions even if they do not purchase anything. Secondly the consumer's name, address and perhaps even phone number – and often additional details as well – are collected for virtually every purchase as a condition of payment by credit card or for shipping purposes.

The computers that log all activities on their systems routinely capture all these particulars. The information ranges from the trivial to the most sensitive. In a typical electronic commerce transaction, this information would include not just the record of the items actually purchased but a list of all other others that were viewed. Companies also often collect information from consumers in exchange for a free service, such. Background as news searches, free email and stock portfolios. In many cases, users are not informed that the information is being collected. Not surprisingly, however, those customer details are frequently fodder for targeting advertising.

Companies such as Netzero offer free net access in exchange for monitoring their users' activities for advertisers. Web sites known as "portals" offer personalised pages where a user can set up a free account to get selected news or stock quotes or chat with other users once they register and provide their names, addresses and interests.

A key concept in online marketing is personalisation. This is the belief that marketers can collect enough information about consumers to determine their desires for goods and to target specific advertising or other services at them. The perceived value of this information is what makes many of these dot.com companies worth so much on the stock market. The companies then sell, trade or share that information among third party companies without the consumer's express knowledge or consent.

Internet security

Internet security also raises serious concerns about privacy. Many web sites that retain personal information are poorly secured against accidental releases or deliberate attempts to penetrate computer systems for fraudulent purposes. 5 At least one major security flaw in common software used by consumers and consumer-oriented businesses is discovered every week. It is common to have security breaches that result in the disclosure of personal information or financial records.

Many electronic commerce companies respond to concerns about security by stating that they are using encryption to scramble the communications between the user and the server – to prevent a third party from eavesdropping – when the user is providing sensitive information. However, this protection is largely illusory. That information is highly vulnerable once it is collected and included on online databases. Leaks of personal and credit card information occur daily, many involving hundreds of thousands of records. Thousands of customers of CD universe had to replace their credit cards after the database was stolen and offered for sale on the internet. In August 2000, Kaiser Permanente, a top US health insurer, admitted that it had compromised the confidentiality and privacy of its members when it sent over 800 email messages, many containing sensitive information, to the wrong members.

In many cases, the consumer is not even aware that the information is on the net. Here are just two frightening examples: in Michigan, health information, including names, social security numbers and diagnostic codes of thousands of patients, was placed on the internet by the University of Michigan health care system and was publicly available for months. The US Social Security administration made their retirement database available on the internet in 1997 without any prior consultation.

Spam

One manifestation of privacy invasions on the internet is the flood of unwanted electronic mail sent to consumers every day. Unsolicited commercial email, commonly known as "spam," is a major nuisance. Each day, millions of unsolicited electronic mails are sent to consumers. The Gartner Group estimates that 90% of all internet users receive one item of spam at least weekly and half receive six or more each week. It is estimated that the average consumer will receive 1,600 spam messages each year by 2005.

Spam is an example of the failure to apply fair information practices. Addresses are purchased from electronic commerce companies and harvested secretly from web pages, discussion groups, and web chats. Consumer consent is not asked before the address is collected, used or transferred. Consumers have few options for reducing this problem. Once a consumer's email address is on a list, it is difficult to remove.

Many spam messages do not have real return addresses. Even if there is a real address, many spammers take return messages to create new lists of verified email addresses that they can sell for a greater amount. It is also difficult to use technical measures to filter out unwanted messages, since they come from thousands of different addresses. Much of the spam now arrives with misleading subjects such as "regarding your message", to encourage consumers to read the email.

Spam clutters up consumers' email boxes and makes it difficult to find important email. Many consumers are forced to change their email addresses and services to avoid spam. Some stop using the internet altogether because they are tired of receiving so much junk. Spam also costs the consumer money. In many areas around the world, the consumer must pay per minute or download charges to either the telephone company or the internet service provider. In addition, many internet service providers have to expend extensive resources hiring staff and buying additional equipment to deal with the flood of electronic mail they receive – and that cost is passed on to their customers.

America Online (AOL) estimates that one-third of incoming mail to its servers – between 10 and 24 million messages each day – is spam. An industry association estimated in 1999 that $2 of each customer's bill could be traced to spam-related costs. Marketers can also use spam to track user activities. Spam that is sent in html form and read by users of AOL or many other common email programs can send messages to advertising networks such as DoubleClick, linking consumers' email addresses with their cookies.

Most of the manufacturers suppressed the number after a consumer boycott was announced, and Intel announced in 2000 that it is dropping the serial number in future chips. Soon after, several companies, including Microsoft and RealAudio, were discovered using the internal networking number found in most computers as another identifier.

The Internet Engineering Task Force has developed specifications for the next version of the Internet's underlying protocols called IPv6 that will assign a unique permanent ID number to every device hooked into the net, which could one day include common household devices such as refrigerators and VCRs. The growing use of wireless devices also raises serious concerns. Several US cellular phone providers disclose the user's phone number as well as their Internet address when a customer uses their phone to access the Internet.

Growing numbers of programmes and devices exist that secretly monitor the activities of the user and send information back to the company that created it. In some cases, the software sends back a unique identifier. In others, such as with RealPlayer, the software sends a unique identifier and detailed information on the music that the user was listening to.

Recently, readers of Wired, Forbes and other magazines were sent a free plug-in bar code scanner called the CueCat. Using the device, users can visit websites by reading bar codes in magazines and newspapers or that are encoded into television shows or ads. At the same time, the devices contain a unique ID number and maintain a detailed database of the users' activities. When hobbyists starting developing their own software that deleted the ID number and bypassed the corporate database, the companies' lawyers threatened them with violating intellectual property.

The convergence of communications networks, computers and mass media into an interactive network combining television and the Internet is the next progression of the technology currently being developed. Slowly, intelligent cable TV boxes, which can use broadband and interactive cable systems, are being deployed in many jurisdictions around the world.

The new systems are being designed, like their Internet predecessors, to track every activity of users as they surf the net through the boxes. They also are being designed to track the shows and commercials users watch and to use that information to tailor advertising for the greatest effect.

The industry calls this "T-Commerce" for Television Commerce. Millions of consumers are expected to be using these in just the next few years, and the ad revenue to justify the new expensive boxes is expected to hit $5 billion by 2004. Media titan Rupert Murdoch said of the box in a recent NewsCorp annual report, "It will tell us not only who the customers are, but what they buy, what they watch, what they read and what they want." Unlike personal computers that give users control over their actions and choices, the new TV systems are generally based on a sealed "black box" controlled by the company that gives the user little or no control.

In the WebTV box, users are not able to refuse cookies or delete them afterwards. The systems are closed and it is difficult, if not impossible, for even advanced users to identify what the system is doing. It will also prevent users from being able to use their own software. Meanwhile, there are other companies that have developed devices that will automatically record television shows for viewers and make recommendations for new shows based on viewers' previous behaviour. These systems also send some information on the viewers' habits back to the central offices.

In the future, advertisers plan to combine marketing with mobile phone location so that marketers will be able to page or message customers on their phones to alert them to shopping opportunities – as they are passing selected restaurants, for example, or a sporting goods store. A more common practice is using spam to offer fraudulent schemes or pornography.

Privacy laws

The legal protection of privacy is deeply rooted in history going back to Biblical times. More recently, countries began adopting laws protecting citizens from the publication of their personal information. France prohibited the publication of private facts and set stiff fines for violators in 1858. The Norwegian criminal code prohibited the publication of information relating to "personal or domestic affairs" in 1889. In 1890, American lawyers Samuel Warren and Louis Brandeis wrote a seminal piece on the right to privacy as a tort action, describing privacy as "the right to be left alone. " Following the publication, this concept of the privacy tort was gradually picked up across the US as part of the common law.

The modern privacy benchmark at an international level can be found in the 1948 Universal Declaration of Human Rights, which specifically protects territorial and communications privacy. It also recognises that individuals have a right to legal protections against invasions of their privacy. Interest in the right of privacy increased in the 1960s and 1970s with the advent of information technology. The surveillance potential of powerful computer systems prompted demands for specific rules governing the collection and handling of personal information.

The genesis of modern legislation in this area can be traced to the first data protection law in the world enacted in the Land of Hesse in Germany in 1970. National laws in Sweden (1973), the United States (1974), Germany (1977), and France (1978) followed this. Today, over 30 countries have comprehensive laws governing the processing and use of personal information. Another 20 countries are actively considering new laws.

Most countries around the world have sectoral laws protecting privacy in some aspect or another. A major milestone was the European Union's adoption of data protection laws in 1995 and 1997, to harmonise laws throughout the EU in order to ensure consistent levels of protections for citizens, and to allow for the free flow of personal information throughout the EU. The Directives set a baseline common level of privacy which not only reinforce current data protection law, but extended it to establish a range of new rights. The 1995 Data Protection Directive set a benchmark for national law for processing personal information in electronic and manual files. The

1997 Telecommunications Directive established specific protections covering telephone, digital television, mobile networks and other telecommunications systems.

In July 2000, the European Commission, issued a proposal for a new directive on "the processing of personal data and the protection of privacy in the electronic communications sector. " It will replace the existing 1997 Telecommunications Directive by extending the existing protections for an individual's "telecommunications" to a broader, more technology-neutral category of "electronic communications." These new provisions would, for example, ensure the protection of all information ("traffic") transmitted across the Internet, prohibit unsolicited commercial marketing by e-mail (spam) without opt-in consent, and protect mobile phone users from precise location tracking and surveillance.

The directive also gives subscribers to all electronic communications services (such as GSM and e-mail) the right to chose whether they are listed in a public directory. In all of the EU efforts, enforceability is a key concept. The EU is concerned that data subjects have rights that are enshrined in explicit rules, and that they can go to a person or an authority empowered to act on their behalf. Every EU country has a Data Protection Commissioner or agency that enforces the rules. It is expected that the countries with which Europe does business will need to provide a similar level of oversight.

The Directive imposes an obligation on Member States to ensure that the personal information relating to European citizens has the same level of protection when it is exported to, and processed in, countries outside the EU. Many countries outside the EU have adopted similar laws. This is especially common in Central and Eastern Europe where the countries are attempting to join the EU and the Council of Europe. Many countries in the Western Hemisphere are also moving forward. In Canada, the Federal Parliament approved Bill C-6, the Personal Information Protection and Electronic Documents Act in April 2000.

The Act adopts the Canadian Standards Association's International Privacy Code into law for enterprises that process personal information "in the course of a commercial activity," and for federally regulated employers with respect to their employees. In three years, the Act will cover provincially regulated sectors unless the province enacts "substantially similar" laws. such as Quebéc's law.

Laws based on the EU Directives have also been approved in Chile and Argentina. In Asia, Hong Kong and Taiwan have already adopted laws and nearly a dozen other countries are actively considering new laws on data protection.

Sectoral Laws

Some countries, such as the United States, have avoided enacting general data protection rules in favour of laws governing specific areas such as medical or financial records. In such cases, enforcement is achieved through a range of mechanisms. A major drawback with this approach is that it requires that new legislation be introduced with each new technology, so protections frequently lag behind. The lack of legal protections for medical and genetic information in the US is a striking example of its limitations. There is also the problem of a lack of an oversight agency. In many countries, sectoral laws are used to complement comprehensive legislation by providing more detailed protections for certain categories of information, such as telecommunications, police files or consumer credit records. Other countries such as South Korea and Mexico have adopted specific laws on electronic commerce that also protect privacy.

Self Regulation

Another possible method for protecting privacy is through industry self-regulation, in which companies and industry bodies establish codes of practice and engage in self-policing. Self-regulation has different meanings in the US and Europe. In the US, which lacks a comprehensive privacy protection law, industry is not required to follow any minimal standards and there is little evidence that the aims of the codes are regularly fulfilled. There is also a serious problem with enforcement.

In Europe, there is discussion of self-regulation, but in the EU context, self-regulation usually means that industry develops codes based on the standards in the national data protection laws and enforcement is ensured by the national data protection agencies. In an effort to promote self-regulation, industry is focusing on adopting website privacy policies that provide some information to consumers on what details are collected and how they are used and disclosed. Most major e-commerce sites in the United States have adopted these policies.

Consumers have found numerous problems with these policies. Of primary concern is that in an unregulated environment such as the United States, there is no minimum standard for the policy. Many of the privacy policies. simply state that they are collecting a great deal of information about users and that they are planning to use that information for unknown purposes at their discretion and disclose that information to an unknown number of outside organisations for unknown reasons.

A number of surveys by the US Federal Trade Commission and independent groups such as EPIC, in addition to this study by Consumers International, have found that most privacy policies do not adequately protect privacy.

Because there is no legal framework, the privacy policies can be changed at will by the company. Bookseller Amazon.com recently changed its policy from promising never to sell the personal information of its customers to notifying users that it may do at some point in the future. DoubleClick went from offering a semi-anonymous system to an attempt to merge their online records with personal information from offline.

Problems also arise when the legal status of a company changes. If a company goes bankrupt or is bought by another company, the privacy protections of the policy are in doubt. The information can also be placed in the public record because it is frequently the only asset of the company. When Living.com filed for bankruptcy, the trustee placed the names and addresses of thousands of customers on the web. Finally, enforcement of privacy policies in countries without laws such as the United States is limited. At best, the consumer can ask the Federal Trade Commission or state Attorney General to enforce the promises. Not surprisingly, this works very infrequently.

Tools are available that can protect the privacy of users in many cases. These technologies are known as "Privacy Enhancing Technologies" (PETs) and include anonymous web browsers, remailers and encryption. The European Commission in 1998 looked as some PETs and stated that the tools would not replace a legal framework but could be used to compliment existing laws. Encryption has become the most important tool for protection against surveillance. A message is scrambled so that only the intended recipient will be able to unscramble, and subsequently read the contents.

Pretty Good Privacy (PGP) is the best-known encryption program and has hundreds of thousands of users, including human rights groups. An open source program called GNU Privacy Guard is being developed as a free replacement that will allow anyone to view the full source of the system to ensure that it does not allow for secret surveillance. "Anonymous remailers" strip identifying information from e-mails and can stop traffic analysis. They have generated opposition from police and intelligence services. In Finland, a popular anonymous remailer had to be shut down due to legal challenges that forced the operator to reveal the name of one of the users.

More advanced tools that merge the functions of anonymous remailers and encryption have also been developed. The Mixmaster anonymous remailers used encryption links between anonymous remailers to hide the identity of the original sender by sending the message randomly through a series of remailers before delivering it to the final destination. Another useful tool allows consumers to browse anonymously. Many of these services also prevent cookies, or applications that can be used to spy on the consumer from being placed on the consumer's computer. The most sophisticated ones, such as Freedom.net, provide a fully encrypted link between the user and secure servers run by the company to prevent wiretapping, and encrypted headers so that users can receive email and browse the Internet without even the company knowing who is using the system.

Users should be aware that not all tools are effective at protecting privacy. A major limitation is that almost none of the tools address the protection of privacy once the information is collected. Encryption is useful for ensuing that personal information is protected in transit but this says nothing about how the information is used by the companies once it collected. Industry also offers many tools that are not privacy-protective.

Many of these systems, such as Microsoft's Passport and the World Wide Web Consortium's (W3C) Platform for Privacy Preferences (P3P), are designed more to facilitate data sharing than to protect users. They are also frequently used by US industry as justification for not passing laws. Marketing hype frequently promotes tools as privacy protective that have nothing to do with privacy. American Express announced in October 2000 its Private Payments program, which would allow for the creation of one-time credit card numbers for online purchases.

Europe and the United States

Consumers International's main objective in coordinating this survey was to compare the experience of consumers in the United States (US) and the European Union (EU) because there are major differences in approaches to regulation. Privacy practices are voluntary and business-led in the US. In the EU, many key consumer rights are enshrined both in EU and national legislation. Consumer organisations have expressed concern that EU consumers could be vulnerable to abuse of their personal data when buying from the US or using US-based websites.

Following the approval of the EU Data Protection Directive, many large American companies worried that they would be cut off from data flows from European countries because of the lack of laws protecting privacy in the US. The US government and industry strongly lobbied the EU and member countries to find the US system adequate. In 1998, the US began negotiating a safe harbour agreement with the EU in order to ensure the continued trans-border flow of personal data. Negotiations on the drafting of the principles lasted nearly two years and were the subject of bitter criticism by privacy and consumer advocates and the European Parliament.

In July 2000, despite the criticisms, the Commission approved the safe harbour agreement. Under safe harbour, US companies can voluntarily self-certify to adhere to a set of privacy principles loosely based on the fair information practices developed by the US Department of Commerce and the European Commission. These companies could then continue to receive personal data from the European Union. US companies have been able to join safe harbour from November 2000. However take-up has been remarkably slow, with only one company reportedly joining up as of early December 2000. There is an open-ended grace period for US signatory companies to implement the principles. The Commission promised to re-open negotiations on the arrangement if the remedies available to European citizens prove inadequate.

There are many concerns that the proposal will not adequately protect consumers. A major weakness of the agreement is enforcement. The agreement rests on a self-regulatory system, whereby companies merely promise not to violate their declared privacy practices. There is little enforcement or systematic review of compliance. Individual consumers have no right to appeal or right to compensation for privacy infringements. The agreement will only apply to companies overseen by the Federal Trade Commission and Department of Transportation and special exceptions are granted for public record information protected by EU law. It does not apply to internet or electronic commerce unless a European electronic commerce company transfers information about its customers to a US company that has signed up to the agreement.

To improve the arrangement, Consumers International recommends several changes. These include:

- the creation of a single point of contact for all consumer complaints with a simplified complaint system
- the establishment of biannual public reports on business compliance and the efficacy of the principles
- the creation of effective penalties including fines, restoration of privacy if possible, and compensation
- the establishment of an international e-commerce body with jurisdiction over privacy that could audit, set standards, promote best practices and publish reports.

Children and internet privacy

Parents, educators and many others have expressed considerable concern regarding the protection of children's privacy on the internet, especially because children are considered a lucrative target market for sales and online advertisers. A groundbreaking report by the Center for Media Education entitled *"Web of deception: threats to children from online marketing"* found that children were being targeted in two ways:

1) invasion of children's privacy through solicitation of personal information and tracking of online computer use; and
2) exploitation of vulnerable, young computer users through new unfair and deceptive forms of advertising.

According to the survey, the sites were demanding detailed personal information including name, address, age and interests. Some sites told children that if they provided their name, address and other personal information, they would receive gifts such as t-shirts and games. Some sites made fun of the children who did not provide the information while allowing those who did to play games. A number of sites demanded detailed financial information about the parents.

Deceptive advertising is of particular concern with children. The report found that advertisers deliberately blurred the lines between advertising and information on children's sites. Advertising logos were often incorporated into cartoon characters designed to appeal to children and encourage them to demand these products.

Even something as apparently benign as companies working with schools to increase online access to children has a negative side. A company called Zapme in cooperation with other corporations including Amazon, Dell, Microsoft, Xerox and Yahoo offered free computers, satellite dishes, and internet access in exchange for gathering information about students. Students were required to get an electronic ID and to provide their names, addresses and telephone numbers. The information was then provided to advertisers who targeted the students with individualised ads. The system was discontinued after a coalition of educators, consumer and privacy groups wrote to all of the governors in the US calling on them to reject the system. Other companies offered money to schools to encourage children to sign up for free accounts on their services.

In the United States, recognising these abuses, the US Congress approved the Children's Online Privacy Protection Act (COPPA) in 1998. The Act requires parental consent before information is collected from children under the age of 13 and allows parents to access information about their child. In order to assess companies' approach to privacy on sites targeting children, Consumers International assessed a small number of children's sites. One hundred and two sites were assessed in the US and EU. The findings indicate that the situation is still very worrying. Whilst a high number of companies are prepared to sell things to children online, very few seem to adhere to good privacy practice.

The findings demonstrated that only a minority of sites (12%) had a clear, easy-to-understand privacy policy; even fewer (10%) asked children to obtain parental consent before disclosing information, asked children to tell parents they had given information to the site, or offered to email parents warning them that data had been disclosed. Although this exercise was small-scale, Consumers International feels this is a strong indication that sites targeting children are performing very poorly in their approach to privacy. This area merits a separate study in its own right.

The survey project was carried out by an international team. Researchers from 14 consumer organisations around the world carried out the assessments. The full team met to discuss the findings and to agree to conclusions and recommendations. The participants were:

Australia	Australian Consumers Association
Belgium	Verbruikersunie
Denmark	Danish Consumer Council/Forb-rugerradet
France	UFC-Que Choisir
Holland	Consumentenbond
Hong Kong	Hong Kong Consumer Council
Japan	Consumer Law News Network
Norway	Norwegian Consumer Council/ Forbrukerradet
Poland	Polish Consumer Federation
Sweden	Konsumentverket
United Kingdom	Consumers Association And National Consumer Council
United States	American Council For Consumer Interests Coordinator Consumers International (ODTE)

The research consisted of a large-scale assessment by users of internet sites. In total, the participants assessed 751 sites, based mainly in the European Union and United States. The objective of the project was to determine the sites' approach to data protection, and therefore researchers concentrated on types of site where consumers would be likely to be asked to divulge personal information when shopping or searching for information. The participants researched retail sites, financial sites, health-related sites and in addition they looked at the most popular or heavily used sites on the web. Researchers also carried out a separate examination of sites targeted at children.

The category of *retail* sites covered businesses selling products to the consumer, and covered a wide range of companies including car dealers and restaurants as well as shops. Not all the sites within this category actually sold products online. Some provided information about their product range, store location, and offered catalogues online.

The *financial* category included banks, insurance companies, money advice sites, online brokers, mortgage companies and credit unions. Not all of these sold their financial products online.

The *health* category included general advice sites, doctors, dentists, and sites specialising in giving advice about one condition, hospitals, retailers of healthcare products, healthcare service providers and others.

The *most popular* category covered a wide range of heavily used sites, including portal sites, email and internet access providers, news sites, weather sites, travel services, magazines, recruitment sites linked to television and radio stations, online directories, and games and leisure sites.

Rather than just visiting and assessing the biggest sites within each category, as this might not give a complete picture of the internet world, the sites were chosen to represent a cross-section of those that consumers would come across when surfing the web.

The project's findings offer a snapshot of the privacy situation on sites run by large, medium and small companies. How sites were selected Dun and Bradstreet, an internet listings firm, created a list of 300 US-based sites and 300 EU-based sites for each of the *retail, financial* and *health* categories.

The project manager selected sites at random from Dun and Bradstreet's listings within each category. The list of EU sites was drawn proportionately to the total number of addresses for each EU country within Dun and Bradstreet's total pool.

Researchers then worked their way down the lists, eliminating any sites that were not aimed at consumers. For the *most popular* category, researchers provided a list of the top 100 sites in their country to the project manager, who then used a process of random selection to create a sample pool for the US and the EU.

Sites were eliminated if they were not aimed at consumers, were pornographic, or were not accessible. For children's sites, the sub-categories within the US site www.yahooligans.com were used and researchers were asked to provide a list of at least ten sites within each sub-category.

The project manager then used random selection to create a sample pool of sites for each country in the study. A total of 751 sites were assessed for the main study.

The sites fell into the following categories:

Health	173
Financial	185
Retail	214
Most Popular	177 (not stated 3)

Sites were based in the following countries:

USA	340
EU	339 of which: UK 83
Denmark	86
France	25
Belgium	10
Germany	83
Sweden	52
Hong Kong	69

In addition, 102 questionnaires were completed about children's sites.

The number of sites assessed during this research is large enough for Consumers International to be able to draw conclusions with confidence about the state of data collection and protection in the US and EU at the time the research was carried out. The assessments were carried out from March to July 2000.

Number of questionnaires completed by each organisation:

Australia	Australian Consumers Association	29
Belgium	Verbruikersunie	9
Denmark	Danish Consumer Council	19
France	UFC-Que Choisir	25
Holland	Consumentenbond	68
Hong Kong	Hong Kong Consumer Council	119
Japan	Consumer Law News Network	65
Norway	Norwegian Consumer Council	92
Poland	Polish Consumer Federation	31
Sweden	Konsumentverket	51
UK	Consumers Association	46
	National Consumer Council	24
US	US Council For Consumer Interests	87
	Consumers' International	86

Consumers International wanted to find out whether it's possible for a consumer to browse sites and gather information without giving away information about him or herself. Consumers International sought to determine what sort of information companies wanted to gather about consumers. Did they want the obvious information such as names and addresses; or did they ask for other details which consumers might consider more personal, such as age or occupation? Did these companies offer a choice about whether to provide this information, or was it compulsory if a customer wanted to use their sites?

Consumers International also wanted to investigate a company's approach to protecting the privacy of consumers' data. Did the company have a privacy policy – a document that explains what it does with a customer's personal information and why? Did it give choices about whether a user wanted to be on the company's mailing list, or whether he or she wanted it to pass private details on to that company's associates or even to other unrelated companies? If the company did have a privacy policy, was it easy to find?

In addition to noting whether or not the company had a privacy policy, researchers assessed those policies, to judge how many of them presented consumers with adequate information and choices. When visiting the site, the researchers established whether the site required consumers to divulge personal information in order to use it. If so, the researchers then completed a detailed questionnaire that looked at what information the site collected; whether it gave choices about what happened to that information; whether the site had a privacy policy; and what was in that privacy policy. The researchers were asked to collect the following information:

- what sort of information the site asked for (e.g. name, address, date of birth, occupation); and whether this was compulsory or optional
- at what stage this information was collected (did a customer have to give this information up-front before he or she could use the site, or only when he or she wanted to buy something or personalise the site)
- whether the site alerted the consumer to the company's privacy policy

- whether the consumer was able to opt out of mailing lists
- whether the site collected personal information in any other ways (e.g. surveys or competitions)
- whether the site had a privacy policy
- how easy it was to find the privacy policy
- what was contained in the privacy policy
- whether the site belonged to any sort of certification scheme
- whether the site explained its use of cookies
- whether the site gave information about security of payment systems

The project's definition of information collection included any request for personal information either before or during the use of the site. Researchers noted any non-transparent methods of information collection such as surveys, competitions and feedback forms, in addition to all transparent methods. However, if the only way a site collected information was by providing an email address for feedback, and that email was voluntary on the part of customers and not related to their use of the site, then that site was classified as not collecting information about the user.

When searching for a privacy policy, researchers started by looking for a clearly-labelled statement that explained what the site did with information collected from the user. This might be called different things in different countries, but researchers were looking for something that explained what information is collected; what is done with that information; who it is shared with; what choices the user has about its use; and how security of that data is ensured. If researchers were unable to find a specific privacy policy, they carried out a key word search if possible. If that still failed to yield any information about the site's approach to privacy, they sent an email to the site asking it what its policy was.

The large-scale assessment of website practices and policies described in the previous section gives a good indication of what companies say they do with the personal information their customers give them. However, this may not always be what happens in practice.

Consumers International wanted to find out whether companies always live up to their promises. In order to test this out, researchers conducted a small investigative research exercise to better understand how privacy is protected and respected in a real internet shopping situation. This exercise is small-scale, so it offers no quantitative indication of website behaviour in general. However it gives valuable insight into potential problem areas.

A small team of researchers created a number of email "identities" to be used solely for this exercise. These researchers then made purchases on a range of sites in the USA and Europe (UK, Germany, France and Denmark). They bought a variety of products including books and CDs, pharmaceutical products, baby goods, chocolates and wine. They also made purchases on sites dedicated to weddings and fan clubs.

Whenever the site gave the consumer choices about including their name on a mailing list, the researcher made two purchases. Each purchase was made as a different person, using the unique email identities established at the outset. For one purchase, the researcher asked not to be included on any mailing lists for follow-up marketing, be it the company's own mailing list, or a third-party list. The researcher would then make a second purchase, using a second identity, and indicate that he or she *was* willing to receive further information in the future.

When a site did not offer a choice, researchers made one purchase only and noted the company's policy on privacy and follow-up marketing. Researchers then assessed whether the companies involved adhered to these requests, by tracking whether the identities received any further information or junk mail. Researchers placed 52 orders in total, using 17 sites in the United States and 16 sites in Europe. Of these sites, 10 offered no choice about marketing follow-up; the rest did offer a choice. Orders were placed in October 2000.

Thye survey conducted by consumer international includes results of any follow-up mail sent until the end of November 2000. Of course, some companies may take some time to send out marketing material, and the process of selling names to third parties who then use those names for marketing purposes may take time as well. So this can only be an interim report, which hopefully will be followed with fuller findings.

The majority of sites that gave consumers choice about whether or not they wanted their details used for mailing lists honoured those choices. Of the 21 identities that indicated they did not want any further information, be it from the company, its affiliates, or third parties, the majority did, in fact, not receive any further mail – be it in electronic or postal format (at least so far). However, in three cases the company disregarded this request and sent their own email advertisements anyway. These sites were www.lalibrairie.com (a French site selling books and CDs), www.healthshop.com (a US site selling health products), and www.bbr.com (a UK wine retailer Berry Bros. & Rudd). www.bbr.com also sent regular mail to this identity. In one case an identity who purchased something from the US CD retailer www.cdnow.com received an email from a third party offering university diplomas for sale, although the same identity did not receive any emails from the company itself. It is possible that this third party site just sent out "blind" emails to names at this respective email provider address. However, none of the other identities using this email provider received a similar solicitation.

By comparison, of the 21 identities that did indicate they were willing to receive further mail of any sort, more than half of them (12) did receive email solicitations from the company itself. Only two received postal solicitations so far – one from www.thenutfactory.com (a US retailer specialising in dried fruits and nuts), and one, again, from www.bbr.com. Not a single one has so far received emails or postal mail from a third party.

Of the 10 identities that were not given a choice, seven did not receive any electronic or postal mail at all, while three did receive email solicitations. These were fom www.harvard.com (a US bookseller), www.babyworld.co.uk (a UK retailer specialising in baby products), and www.rouge-blanc.com (a French wine retailer).

The conclusion reached by this exercise is that whatever a website's privacy policy might say, a consumer cannot be absolutely confident that in all cases the site will adhere to this policy. In three out of 21 cases, websites used the customer's personal details for marketing purposes despite the fact that the customer had explicitly chosen not to receive any such information. These results are based on monitoring over a short period – as time goes on, Consumers International may find even more companies breaching their promises to their customers.

A special opt-out procedure that seems to appear on many French websites raised an interesting point. The procedures made it very cumbersome for consumers to act on their right to opt out of mailing lists. Several of the sites tested did not provide the usual method of opting out of further emails – by ticking a certain box, for example, while placing an order. Instead, at some point during the transaction, the sites alerted consumers, although rarely in a prominent place, to their rights under Article 36 of the French Information & Liberty Law of 1978.

In order to prevent a company from using the consumer's information or from sending him or her further information in the future, it is necessary to send a postal letter to the company. This was the case with the sites www.lalibrairie.com and www.avecbebe.com. The two French sites www.rouge-blanc.com and www.nature-bio. com, notably did not make a reference to this law on their websites, nor did they provide opt-out choices. Researchers also uncovered some worrying findings regarding security of payment card information. Researchers encountered various sites that did not have secure connections for the transmission of credit card and other personal details.

Two of the most alarming examples involved two US sites. In one case, www.3tee.com (a US t-shirt retailer) requested further information before finalising the order, through an un-encrypted email that included all the credit card and personal information the consumer had provided when placing the order (although the order itself was placed through an encrypted system). In another case, the US CD retailer www.cdworld.com sent out two emails requesting further credit card confirmation details to be faxed to the company. They said they would not process the order unless they received this additional verification. However, in spite of the fact that researchers did not provide the company with this further verification, processed the order eventually.

Interestingly, when the second identity placed the same order, using the same payment method, the company never requested further verification .

Just over two thirds of the sites assessed (67%) collected some sort of personal information about the visitor, at some point during the visit. Just under a third (32%) of the sites didn't ask for any information at any point during the visit. Sites within the *most popular* category were most likely to gather something from the user, with 74% of sites visited collecting certain details. Sites within the *retail* and *financial* categories were close behind, with 73% and 70% of sites respectively gathering information. *Health* sites were least likely to collect anything, with 50% asking for information.

While the total percentage of sites collecting information is similar across the US and EU, there are some differences between findings for the US and EU sites within the categories. US-based *financial* sites are much more likely to collect information than EU-based *financial* sites. Researchers found that the US *financial* sites were much more likely to offer products and allow customers to apply online, which accounts for some of the difference.

Within the *retail* category, many of the sites within the US sample were websites for local businesses (such as car dealers or restaurants) that gave details of their products but did not allow consumers to actually buy online.

These type of sites did not appear as frequently in the EU *retail* sample. This explains why the sites in the US *retail* sample are less likely to collect personal data than the sites in the EU *retail* category.

Table 1: site collects information

Total	*US%*	*EU%*
Most popular	80	72
Financial	84	48
Retail	61	79
Health	47	47
Overall total	***66***	***63***

Site tried to place cookie on the computer Consumers International asked the researchers to set their browsers to alert them every time a cookie was placed. Just over a third of the sites visited tried to place at least one cookie.

The vast majority of sites just placed one or two cookies, but a few placed up to fifty.US *most popular* sites were most likely to place cookies, with 92% of these sites visited in the survey placing at least one cookie.

Table 2: site placed at least one cookie

	US%	EU%
Most popular	92	47
Financial	22	24
Retail	30	32
Health	22	15

Almost all sites (99%) that gathered information collected some detail that would enable them to identify a user personally (for example, name, address, credit or social security card number). US *most popular* sites were the least likely to do this with 87.5% collecting something personally identifiable; all other categories did this between 96% and 100% of cases. Many sites also collected information that would enable them to know something about the user (and therefore possibly his or her spending habits), such as where you live, your address, age or occupation. In this way, many sites are able to build a profile of the customer in order to target their marketing activities.

Name, email name, and postal address details were the most commonly collected information across all sites. Age or date of birth, occupation, gender, fax details and credit card details were the other sorts of information that sites collected. If a site collected information at all, it was quite likely to request a substantial amount of information from the consumer. Most sites collected between six and eight pieces of information. At what stage was the information collected? Only 15 of the sites researchers visited, or 7% of the total, insisted on receiving information before allowing a customer to visit the site.

It was most common to collect information after the user browsed the site, but before he or she made a purchase or requested specific information. This was true across all types of site, and is not surprising as many sites need to know certain things about the customer in order to respond to orders or requests.

US-based *most popular* sites were most likely to collect information before letting a user use the site – although this only happened in a minority of cases. The most-commonly asked question, appearing on 15 sites, was what country the customer was based in. This could be because the company needs to adapt the site in order to make it applicable to the country in which the user is located.

After searching thoroughly on each site, researchers were able to find a privacy policy for 292 (58%) of the sites visited that collected personal information. Of sites that collected personal information from users, *health* sites were the least likely to have a privacy policy. US-based *most popular* sites were most likely to have a privacy policy, with all sites assessed in the study containing a privacy policy of some sort. Most *popular* sites within EU and US-based financial sites also performed well.

Did the site alert the user to its privacy policy at the point where the information was collected?

If a site has a policy that explains what it does with the information supplied by the customer, the most obvious place to alert users to this is at the point where information is collected, rather than leave the user to hunt around for it. Only a third (32.5%) of the sites that collected personal information and had a privacy policy bothered to alert the visitor to the privacy policy at the point where that information was collected. The only category of site that performed well in this respect was US-based *most popular* sites. Nearly two-thirds (62.5%) of these sites with privacy policies alerted users to them at the point where the information was collected.

How easy was it to find the privacy policy?

If a company has a privacy policy, supposedly for the benefit of consumers, it makes sense for this policy to be easily accessible. It is of little use to consumers if they cannot find it at the point when they need to read it. Ideally the privacy policy should be clearly sign-posted from the home page, in addition to being clearly marked at any point where data is collected from the user. However researchers found that this only happened in a minority of cases.

Researchers were signposted to the privacy policy from the home page in over a third (39%) of cases where sites collected information and had a privacy policy. US sites fared better than EU sites. In particular, *most popular* sites based in the US did far better than any other category – 97.5% of sites signposted their policies clearly.

Even when the privacy policy was signposted from the home page, it wasn't always easy to find. Researchers found that the privacy policy was prominent and easy to find in 63% of those sites where the policy was signposted from the home page – leaving 37% to do better.

If the privacy policy was not signposted from the home page, researchers were asked to attempt to find it by clicking around the site. One in five (20.5%) managed to find the privacy policy this way. If they were still unable to find the privacy policy by clicking around the site, they proceeded to search within the site, using a search facility, if one existed. Although 18.5% of sites without an apparent privacy policy had a search facility, researchers only managed to find a privacy policy this way in two cases.

If, after all this searching, the researchers were still unable to locate a privacy policy, they emailed the sites to ask if they had a privacy policy. Researchers sent 177 emails inquiring if a privacy policy existed. Only 30 sites, or 17% responded. The sites' low response reflects a very poor performance, given the high level of consumer concern over privacy of personal data. As prompt response to emails is an essential part of building consumer faith in electronic commerce, it shows that many sites still have a long way to go to provide good customer service. When companies did respond to the emails, the answers varied.

The following responses are the most typical:

- the data is treated confidentially
- the data is not collected for any marketing purposes
- the data is not stored.

Some sites misunderstood the question and gave answers that related to the way they encrypted data to ensure secure transmission. A few sites said they had plans to post a privacy statement on their site in the near future.

Were users given a choice about what purposes their data could be used for?

Companies may use customers' details for marketing purposes in a number of different ways. They may want to put those details on their own internal mailing list, in order to be able to send information about special offers or new products. They may want to pass the customer's name on to affiliates or associated companies. Or they might want to sell the customer's name as part of a list to an outside company. Ideally consumers should be given the choice of opting in or out of all of these lists. Some companies have a stated policy of not passing personal details on to any other company, affiliated or otherwise. Nonetheless, they should still give consumers the option of not receiving promotional material from them.

European Union law requires companies that plan to use consumers' data for marketing purposes to give them the option of opting-out of this usage. There is no such requirement in the US. Despite this difference in legal requirement, researchers found that in general US-based sites were more likely to give users a choice about whether they wanted their details used or passed on for marketing purposes.

In general sites within the *most popular* category tended to perform better than other types of sites, both in the US and the EU. US-based *most popular* sites performed best of all. However all sites were very disappointing in the extremely low levels of choice given to users.

Did the site give you a choice about having your details put on their own mailing list?

Yes 20% No 80%

The only category that did relatively well was US *most popular* sites.

Did the site give you a choice about affiliates' mailing lists?

Yes 9% No 91%

Again US *most popular* sites did best (42.5% gave a choice)

Did the site give you a choice about third parties' mailing lists?

Yes 9.5% No 87% N/A 3.5%

Again US *most popular* sites did best (47.5% gave a choice)

Where were the opt-out choices given?

Information about the choices available to the consumer about how personal details are used should be accessible and transparent. These choices should ideally be presented prominently at the point where the user is asked for the information. Many users may not be aware that they might have a choice, so they might not look for such information. Less than half (48%) of the small number of sites that gave opt-out choices offered them at the point where the data was collected. In just over a third (37%) of cases, researchers had to go into the privacy policy in order to find the opt-out choices.

Were other methods used to collect personal information?

Seventy-six (15%) sites attempted to collect data in other ways. Companies used competitions as the most common method of collecting information. Other methods included: surveys or feedback forms; invitations to send email comments on the site; and facilities to order a catalogue or join a club. Such methods of data collection can be a cause for concern if consumers are not clearly warned that personal information collected in this way will be stored and used by the site.

Certification schemes

Certification schemes are one effort to increase confidence in consumers shopping online. These schemes are essentially a stamp of approval or label given to internet sites which indicate that the companies operate within a certain set of approved standards. Some certification schemes are run by the industry, while others are independent and consumer-led. These "stamps of approval" should provide consumers with the confidence that they are shopping in a relatively safe environment.

Very few of the sites assessed in the study were part of a certification scheme. Those that were part of a certification scheme were almost all based in the US, where such certification programmes have existed for a longer time. Sample sizes are too low to allow any comment on whether belonging to a certification scheme improves the site's approach to privacy.

Content of privacy policy

Although having some sort of statement about what a site does with information is probably better than having nothing at all, many privacy policies are woefully inadequate. For users to be fully informed, the site should tell them: what information is collected and how it is used; what choices users have about the use of that data; what access users have to the data and how to amend it; how the security of that data is ensured; and who in the organisation is responsible for the data.

Researchers also looked to see whether sites told consumers how long they kept the data, and how their policy might change in the future. Although a site might have a very good privacy policy at the time the consumer uses the site, it could change in the future either because of a change of internal policy, or because that site gets taken over by another company. Ideally sites should warn customers of this possibility, and explain how they would inform the user of any significant changes to policy.

Whenever researchers came across a site with a privacy policy of any sort, they searched for these key aspects within the policy. Within this section, percentages refer to the total number of sites that both collected information about their users, and had some sort of privacy policy. Researchers found that the content of privacy policies was very similar in both US and EU-based sites.

Information

What information is gathered about the customer?

Overall 39% of policies told customers this.

most popular	54%
financial	36%
retail	28%
health	17%

What is done with the information?

This was the most common feature of privacy policies of both US and EU-based sites, with 52% of policies giving information about this.

most popular	69%
financial	47%
retail	42%
health	33%

Why is information gathered about the customer?

This was the second-most-common feature of privacy policies of US and EU-based sites, with 48% of sites covering it.

most popular	61%
financial	49%
retail	35%
health	23%

Who is the information shared with and for what purpose?

Overall 42.5% of site policies covered this.

most popular	54%
financial	42%
retail	32%
health	22%

Choice

What choices are available to customers about what is done with their personal information?

Overall 17.5% told users about the options available to them.

most popular	26%
financial	16%
retail	12%
health	0

Can customers take their names off mailing lists in the future, and if so, how?

Overall 14% informed customers about this.

most popular	13%
financial	14%
retail	11%
health	17%.

Access

Can consumers correct and update information about themselves, and if so how?

Overall 31% included this in their policies.

most popular	44%
financial	26%
retail	22%
health	22%

Can customers access information held about them, and if so, how?

Overall 18% of site policies covered this.

most popular	17%
financial	20.5%
retail	17%
health 11	%

Can customers delete information, and if so, how?

Overall 16% of sites contained information about this.

most popular	24%
financial	11%
retail	11%
health	11%

Security

How is data security managed?

Overall 22% of site policies covered this.

most popular	20%
financial	26%
retail	22%
health	6%

Other aspects: Is the name of the person responsible for data provided?

Overall 5% of policies included this.

most popular	6%
financial	4.5%
retail	5%
health	0

How long is information held for?

Overall 6% of policies included this.

most popular	8%
financial	0%
retail	7%
health	17%

Is there any guarantee of how long the site's policy will remain unchanged/might change in the future?

Overall 4% of policies included this.

most popular	5%
financial	4.5%
retail	2.5%
health	0

Generally the numbers of sites providing any of this key information were very low. Only US-based *most popular* sites stood out from the rest, with 88% telling the user what information is gathered about them; 85% saying why that information is gathered; 90% telling consumers what is done with that information; 78% telling consumers who that information is shared with and 66% telling consumers how to correct or update that information. In all other categories, sites performed very badly, with the vast majority failing to meet any of the important criteria needed for an adequate privacy policy. This leads to the worrying conclusion that only a minority of sites that collect information actually tell the user anything about what the companies do with that information. Even when a policy is provided, in many cases it does not offer consumers the key information they need. This failure on the part of the majority of sites is deeply worrying and, particularly since the guidelines on fair information practices in this area are well-established, shows a flagrant disregard for the concerns of consumers. Unless internet sites take a careful look at their privacy policies, they may well see consumer confidence – and willingness to use online services – erode over time.

Electronic commerce companies use numerous methods to identify and track consumers. One of the most common techniques currently used is the cookie. A cookie is a small file that is placed on a user's hard drive by a website. It contains a unique number generated by the site. The number is typically a series of numbers and letters intelligible only to the site but it may also contain the user's account name and password or Internet address.

Cookies were created by Netscape, an internet browser and server company, to improve websites' ability to track users over a single visit to a site. The cookie can also notify the site that the user has returned and can allow the site to track the user's activities across many different visits. The use of cookies expanded greatly when it was realised that a single cookie could be used across many different sites by sending the cookie from a single third-party site. This led to the development of advertising network companies that track which users view which websites and develop profiles of their interests across many sites. These companies then use that information to target specific advertising.

The cookies are not typically associated with a real identity. The largest ad service is DoubleClick, which has agreements with over 11,000 websites and maintains cookies on 100 million users, each linking to hundreds of pieces of information about the user's browsing habits. In 1999, DoubleClick bought a major US offline direct marketing firm and announced that it was going to start merging offline marketing data and user profiles. That announcement resulted in a storm of controversy and the plan has been stopped for the time being. It also was revealed that DoubleClick received information about sensitive information – including health and financial details – about users through the placement of cookies.

A more secretive manner of tracking Internet users involves the use of web bugs, which are invisible images that also place cookies or report back that a user has visited a web site or read a specially formatted email. As of July 2000, DoubleClick had placed web bugs on over 60,000 different web pages. The bugs can also be used to merge cookies with email addresses. There are more permanent methods of identifying users. In 1999, Intel announced that it was including a serial number in each new Pentium III chip that could be accessed by websites and internal corporate networks.

Policy Frameworks for Electronic Commerce

Whereas data-processing systems are designed to serve man, they must, whatever the nationality or residence of natural persons, respect their fundamental rights and freedoms, notably the right to privacy, and contribute to economic and social progress, trade expansion and the well-being of individuals. In developing regulatory and policy frameworks for electronic commerce, Australia has punched above its weight internationally.

As the New Zealand Law Commission recently noted, 'business benefits are to be gained by trading through electronic, rather than paper-based, means'.These business benefits include: lower information transfer costs, lower procurement costs, product customisation, the ability to conduct business over long distances with ease and increased operational efficiency. Similar benefits will apply to the delivery of legal services, particularly in the areas of online service delivery, electronic document lodgement and online access to legal information. The main legal issues that arise in electronic commerce relate to identity and the security and privacy of electronically transmitted and stored information. These issues include how to:

(a) ensure that a person who purports to electronically sign and/or lodge a document is in fact the person who signed and/or lodged the document;

(b) ensure that the document sent by a person is received and stored in the same form in which it was sent;

(c) prevent unauthorised access to documents during transmission and once stored.

The proposed Electronic Commerce Framework Bill seeks to address these issues by establishing a safe and secure legislative framework for the conduct of web-commerce. The proposed Data Protection Bill addresses privacy issues in the context of unauthorised access to and misuse of electronically stored data.

Privacy issues

The risks of conducting business electronically are mainly associated with issues concerning 'identifying parties and the ability of parties to deny transactions' and 'other issues [including] invasion of privacy and loss of confidentiality of communications'.

Consequently, it is important that there is some method by which the author of an electronic document can be reliably ascertained or verified. This can be achieved through the use of electronic signatures and biometric identifiers.

The concept of electronic signatures may be only an intermediate phase as more sophisticated methods of identification will be developed.

Moreover, for an electronic document to be relied upon as authentic, it is essential to be able to demonstrate with a high degree of certainty that a document has not been tampered with or altered in some way. This is particularly important for the electronic lodgement of court documents.

In addressing these issues, the Victorian Government has drafted a proposed Electronic Commerce Framework Bill and circulated it for comment.The bill was developed by the Electronic Commerce Framework Group within Multimedia Victoria, which was chaired by Mr. Victor Perton MP. The bill aims to:

(a) provide legislative recognition of electronic signatures in order to promote and encourage electronic commerce;

(b) encourage the development of industry codes of practice in relation to electronic commerce; and

(c) address issues of computer crime.

The bill is based on international best practice in the regulation of web-commerce including principles expounded by the United Nations Commission on International Trade Law and the policies espoused by OECD member states including, Canada and the United States.

Security of data needs to be addressed at all levels—organisational, governmental and international. So far as organisations are concerned, the implementation of network security, such as access controls and firewalls, and the encryption of data stored and exchanged, are vital to the integrity of an electronic legal system.But beyond the organisational level, there is a need for governments to establish a safe environment for the storage and exchange of data. This can be achieved to a large extent by the use of electronic signatures issued through a 'trusted third party' or certification authority. This method 'is widely acknowledged by governments and the private sector as a cornerstone of trust in electronic commerce'.

Digital Signature

In general terms, a certification authority will issue each party to a transaction with a digital private key and a digital public key. These keys are based on asymmetric cryptography whereby a unique number is created by a mathematical security algorithm. The contractual documents may specify the certifying authority to be used. A party electronically transmitting a document will double encrypt the document using his or her private key and the recipient's public key. The party receiving the document will be in possession of his or her private key and the transmitting party's public key.

If the document is authentic and has not been tampered with, the recipient's private key and the transmitting party's public key will 'unlock' the document and therefore authenticate both the identity of the sender and the integrity of the document. Otherwise, the document will be a meaningless jumble of characters. In Australia the accounting firm KPMG Australia and the credit agency Dunn and Bradstreet jointly offer these services. Australia Post until recently also offered this service through 'KeyPOST', but has withdrawn from the market.

Internationally, these services are provided by a number of organisations including Bureau Veritas Quality International (headquartered in the United Kingdom and with offices in 45 countries), Det Norske Veritas (headquartered in Norway and has 300 offices in 100 countries) and Lloyd's Register of the United Kingdom.

Owing to the fact that technology is advancing at a very rapid rate, there is widespread concern that a form of encryption that is one hundred percent safe today, may become no obstacle to hackers of tomorrow. Although this is a problem for paper-based documents also, the implications of this for the long-term electronic storage of documents cannot be overstated.

One way of protecting the integrity of stored documents is to use a program which constantly 'relocks' the data using the latest technology—in a manner somewhat akin to a virus scanner. This will be effective as long as the other party to the transaction does the same. Both copies of a contract will remain in their original condition. However, if there is a dispute regarding the terms and conditions of an electronically executed contract, each party is capable of producing a different version. It may be possible for an expert to ascertain which is the authentic version, but alternatively it may not, particularly if the contract was 'written' using obsolete technology.

Accordingly, there is a role for an organisation that would be a repository for authentic copies of commercial documents. Such an organisation would need to be above reproach, have extremely long-term viability and very large computer storage facilities. There is a role for the Victorian Government in providing such a 'trusted third party' registry and storage facility on a fee for service basis, at least in the early stages of the development of the information economy.

A substantial Victoria Government electronic registry system presently operates in the Land Registry and the Public Records Office of Victoria has recently published its important report on the Victorian Electronic Records Strategy, establishing international standards for the long-term storage of electronic records.

Such a Government service could significantly assist the process of attracting electronic commerce to Victoria. A condition of use of the registry might be that the contract be subject to Victorian law. Thus, if the registry became internationally renowned for its security and reliability, it could also be a boost to the legal services industry because Victorian law would become 'the law of the contract' in many international contracts, thereby vesting Victorian courts with jurisdiction.

Under the proposed Electronic Commerce Framework Bill, an 'electronic signature' is applied to a document by a person to authenticate the document and to acknowledge that it is being signed. Subject to some exclusions, an electronic signature may be used and is effective for any purpose for which a signature is required or permitted by law.

Subject to the same exclusions, the bill also makes writing in electronic form effective for all purposes, provided 'the electronic form is such as to permit retention of the writing for subsequent reference'. To come within this provision, an electronic document must be such as to permit 'reproduction of the document at any time as it existed when used for the relevant purpose'.This raises the issue noted above of the need to store documents in a tamper-proof manner over lengthy periods of time.

Under the bill, documents may be effectively 'delivered' electronically. There are detailed provisions as to when a document is deemed to have been sent and received.

The provisions of the bill do not apply to certain classes of documents including: testamentary instruments, trust deeds, powers of attorney, documents requiring personal service, affidavits and other sworn documents, or documents required for the creation or transmission of interests in real property.

The view has been expressed that the community is not yet ready for electronic documents in these categories. At this stage, the bill does not extend to documents required or permitted under a law 'regulating the practice or procedure of a court or tribunal'.

Consequently, court documents are presently excluded from the operation of the proposed bill, however, once courts and are able to properly handle the receipt and storage of electronically written, signed and delivered documents, it is probable that this exclusion would be removed.

The bill provides further for the Minister responsible for the legislation to approve:

> any organisation or code of practice that the Minister considers can provide guidance to participants in electronic commerce or facilitate electronic commerce.

This is consistent with the Victorian Government's expressed policy, which is to:

> allow the private sector to lead in the implementation of public key technology, and to create an environment in which information industries can flourish. The Victorian Government through Multimedia Victoria will provide light-handed encouragement of online authentication, by projects such as ESRB [Electronic Signature Recognition Body], in conjunction with education, access and networking programs.

Finally, the bill introduces a number of new offences relating to computers into the Crimes Act 1958 (Vic.), including 'unlawful access to data in a computer' and 'damaging data in a computer'. Both offences can incur a maximum penalty of ten years imprisonment.

The bill is in its final drafting stages, and may be introduced into State Parliament during 1999.

Commonwealth Government Initiatives

Although the Victorian Government has vigorously pursued the need for a State legislative framework for electronic commerce, it 'strongly supports the establishment of an appropriate regulatory framework at a national level by monitoring industry developments and supporting suitable federal initiatives'.Indeed, the federal Attorney-General has said that 'all [Australian] Governments, through their involvement with the Online Council, have expressed their strong desire to rapidly and effectively develop the information economy in Australia'.The Standing Committee of Attorneys-General has recognised also 'the need for swift, cooperative and uniform action to encourage the information economy in Australia to grow'.

As part of a partnership between all Australian governments, the Commonwealth has developed a proposal for a national uniform legislative scheme. The scheme requires all governments to enact legislation within their jurisdiction to facilitate the removal of existing legal impediments to electronic commerce. 'It is the Commonwealth's expectation that the State and Territory legislation will mirror the Electronic Transactions Bill, which is the first component of the national scheme.'However, while it is part of the national scheme, the Commonwealth's bill will operate independently of legislation in other jurisdictions and will take effect immediately from its commencement.

At a meeting in October 1998 of the Standing Committee of Attorneys-General, the Ministers for the States and Territories agreed in principle to a proposal put forward by the federal Attorney-General that 'the Commonwealth proceed to develop uniform legislation to remove legal obstacles to electronic commerce'. Subsequently, in January 1999, the Commonwealth Attorney-General launched an exposure draft Electronic Transactions Bill together with an explanatory paper.

The Electronic Transactions Bill meets the Prime Minister's commitment 'to develop a light-handed regulatory framework for the online environment to support and encourage business and consumer confidence'.The federal Attorney-General has commented that:

> This legislation is not intended to be internet regulation as such, and it should not be seen as restrictive. Rather, the legislation aims to remove existing impediments to electronic commerce. It is permissive in its approach and encourages the opening of new vistas for commerce.

The bill is part of the Commonwealth Government's strategic framework for the development of the information economy in Australia. It will apply to all Commonwealth law--legal requirements under State and Territory law being left to their respective legislatures to enact complementary legislation.It aims to encourage the development of the information economy and in particular the use in commerce of electronic communications. The bill will provide a mechanism for business and the community to voluntarily choose electronic communications when dealing with Commonwealth Government agencies.

Moreover, the bill is intended to facilitate the development of electronic commerce in Australia by removing a number of existing legal impediments to the use of electronic communications. It will put electronic documents and paper-based documents on the same legal footing, in the sense that electronic documents shall not be discriminated against merely because they are in electronic form. Moreover, the bill does not discriminate between different forms of technology.

However, electronic communications can only satisfy legal requirements if they comply with certain specified criteria designed to ensure that the electronic communications are accessible, reliable and maintain the integrity of the information communicated. It should be emphasised that the provisions of the bill are not intended to alter existing legal rights or obligations. Instead, they are designed to allow compliance with existing legal requirements by electronic means.

Like its Victorian counterpart, the Commonwealth draft bill is based on the Model Law on Electronic Commerce prepared by the United Nations Commission on International Trade Law (UNCITRAL), with some modifications recommended by the Federal Government's Electronic Commerce Expert Group.It is intended that the bill be introduced in two stages. Prior to 1 July 2001, it will only apply to Commonwealth laws specified in regulations. After that date, the bill will apply to all laws of the Commonwealth, unless they have been specifically excluded from its application.

The bill is based on two fundamental principles—technology neutrality and media neutrality. 'Technology neutrality' ensures that the law does not discriminate between different forms of technology. 'Media neutrality' means that paper-based commerce and electronic commerce should be treated equally by the law.Consistent with the principle of technology neutrality, the bill does not contain a detailed electronic signature regime, because most electronic signature schemes are technology specific.

In general, the bill provides that any existing requirements under a law of the Commonwealth for writing, signature, the production of documents, and the recording and retention of information can be satisfied by the use of an electronic communication containing the required information, subject to the electronic communication complying with certain specified criteria. Firstly, the method of communicating or generating the information must provide a reasonable means of assuring the maintenance of the integrity of the information contained in the document. Also, the information must be readily accessible so as to be useable for subsequent reference. There is also a requirement that the information comply with particular software or electronic communication specifications, and a requirement that particular action be taken by way of verifying the receipt of the information.

So far as electronic signatures are concerned, the method a person uses to satisfy the requirement must both identify the person and signify their approval of the contents of the electronic communication. It should be noted that, although some signature technologies, such as digital signatures, will by the nature of the way they operate also verify the integrity of the communication, the signature method specified in the bill is not required to verify the integrity of the communication.

The term 'law of the Commonwealth' is not defined in the bill, but is intended to be read in its broadest sense as including all laws of the Commonwealth, whether they are made by or under a statute or derive from the common law or rules of equity. A transitional provision provides that before 1 July 2001 'law of the Commonwealth' means 'a law of the Commonwealth specified in the regulations'.

The bill also sets out default rules intended to operate in the absence of any agreement between the parties to a transaction. These rules deal with the time and place of dispatch and receipt of electronic communications, and the attribution of electronic communications. Specified transactions and/or laws of the Commonwealth can be exempted from the operation of the Act by regulation. Importantly for the purposes of the present Inquiry, Rules of Court made under a law of the Commonwealth may provide that the provisions of the bill do not apply to requirements or permissions that arise under those rules or in connection with the procedures of the courts concerned.

Commonwealth Government Public Key Authority

The Commonwealth Government has established its own peak body known as the Government Public Key Authority (GPKA) for authentication requirements within government and with government clients. The GPKA is responsible for overseeing the use of public and private key technology in government, the application of standards and the evaluation of authentication technologies and service providers.It has established a number of working groups which are considering a wide range of issues including: interoperability of computer systems, privacy issues, confidentiality, non-repudiation of electronic transactions, integrity, ease of use, marketability and archiving of electronic documents, security requirements and technical standards.

National Authentication Authority

The National Office for the Information Economy (NOIE) released a discussion paper in August 1998 containing a proposal for a National Authentication Authority (NAA). NOIE is the Australian Government body responsible for developing strategies to address the key issues arising from the convergence of the information economy, information technology and telecommunications. The NAA proposal is currently awaiting federal cabinet approval.

The NAA would be created to 'facilitate the uptake of authentication and electronic commerce technologies by increasing consumer and business confidence in their use'. Many of the functions proposed for the NAA are similar to those planned for Multimedia Victorian's Electronic Signature Recognition Body. The NAA would aim to reassure consumers and industry of the safety of documents by:

(a) according a 'quality label' to best practice organisations and systems;

(b) endorsing industry developed codes of practice;

(c) recognising relevant industry standards; and

(d) raising awareness of authentication technologies.

The rationale for the creation of a NAA has been explained as follows:

> the NAA would provide independent reassurance that providers of authentication services meet international best practice standards, but in a way that did not constrain the market in its search for viable technologies and business models. The incentive for businesses to have themselves and/or their systems and/or their technologies approved by the NAA would be increased user acceptance and increased marketability.

The Victorian Government is committed to the progress of the Electronic Signature Recognition Body in the absence of any suitable national model, but is prepared to modify its proposals as necessary in order to achieve national uniformity.

Privacy Issues

Privacy issues are crucial in the development of electronic commerce. They have become even more crucial as a result of modern techniques of data storage and 'data mining'. Today's technologies have already led to the storage of vast quantities of data related to us as consumers, taxpayers and web-users. The challenge of the Information Age is that with almost every transaction we leave a data trail which provides a detailed electronic record of our personal history and preferences.

The computerisation of our health, education, employment and consumer records, along with fast improving techniques for the merging of data and the application of profiling, means that frighteningly accurate psychological profiles can now be created on most of us. This information may be sent across state and national boundaries where it can be sold, reused or integrated with other databases without our knowledge or consent.

Privacy and human dignity are the values at the foundation of the secret ballot (as in last Saturday's Federal election), in doctor-patient confidentiality, solicitor-client privilege, even the concept that 'my home is my castle'. The Information Revolution is challenging these very concepts that we tend to take for granted. Yet, given the right legal framework, the price of progress need not be a loss of privacy.

Privacy concerns are one of the major impediments to the take up of the online economy. The April 1998 report by Anderson Consulting, entitled eCommerce: Our Future Today, identified the lack of privacy laws as a significant impediment to the growth of web-commerce. The Federal Privacy Commissioner, Moira Scollay, has stated:

> One of these (impediments) is consumer concern, and producer caution, about the privacy of information transmitted across the Internet or fed into other electronic commerce systems. What will it be used for, where will it end up, what if it is incorrect or misinterpreted? Who else will have access to this information and what will they do with it?

Unauthorised access to information is a significant concern. For example, often in the course of litigation, information of a personal nature is disclosed, such as business, family or medical details. A natural concern of parties revealing such information will be to ensure that it is only used for a specific purpose and not unnecessarily disclosed or accessed. The potential for the unauthorised use of sensitive information is of increased concern where it is stored and transmitted electronically. This is due in part to the greater amount of information that is able to be stored and accessed electronically, and also to a community perception that material stored electronically is less secure than that stored in hardcopy form.

Issues of privacy also arise in the context of the electronic publication of some legal information. For example, although legal decisions and trial transcripts are in the public domain, the greater accessibility to these documents that technology offers may mean that personal information contained within them is more readily accessible and more widely disseminated.

For example, the transcript of the evidence and cross-examination of an alleged rape victim may contain very personal and intimate details, which the victim might not want his or her next door neighbour to read on the Internet. Of course, there is nothing to prevent the curious coming into an open court and listening to the evidence. However, the practicalities of the situation are that this is a less likely scenario than people surfing the web in the privacy of their homes. The result of greater public access to sensitive information is that people may become less willing to provide it. This could have dire consequences for the administration of justice.

It is important that concerns such as these are adequately addressed in order to guarantee the integrity of any electronically facilitated legal system and to establish confidence in the reliability of the system. Without sufficient guarantees of security and a respect for the privacy of information, the development of electronic legal procedures is unlikely to be readily accepted by the legal profession and the wider community.

Security and privacy issues arise in a number of contexts, including the unauthorised interception of electronically transmitted data and unauthorised access to and/or interference with electronically stored data.

Interception

In a system involving electronic document transmission and lodgement, documents may be exchanged between numerous parties and computer systems. These include transmissions between clients, legal practitioners and the court and transmissions between individuals within a legal practice or client company. Modes of document transmission may range from the exchange of floppy disks or CDROMS, transfer via a local area network or intranet, transfer via a wide area network or extranet, to transfer via the Internet.

The possibility of interception of electronic communications in the context of an electronic filing system has the potential to limit its capacity to serve those involved in legal proceedings. This is particularly so where there is the potential for the disclosure of confidential client/legal practitioner communications, which could have a significantly detrimental effect on the conduct of actual or contemplated legal proceedings. The risk of interception also reduces confidence in the authenticity of any communication. Without sufficient safeguards, court processes could be seriously degraded.

Where communication is by the exchange of floppy disks or CD Roms, the risk of interception may be no greater than is currently the case with traditional forms of communication.Where information is exchanged over a computer network, the communication is conducted over shared communication lines. This means that it is possible for an outsider to program their computer system to receive copies of messages exchanged between two parties.

It is also possible for an outsider to configure their computer to emulate that of the intended recipient of a message. This would allow a third party to act as an impostor and to intercept messages intended for the recipient. The imposter could also reply to the sender in the name of the intended recipient, giving the impression that the message was properly received. The proposed legislation previously discussed under 'Security Issues' goes some way towards overcoming these problems.

Even if the outsider cannot view the contents of the message, he or she may still be able to determine attributes of the communication such as the time, amount of information exchanged and the parties involved. This may be significant in the context of some commercially sensitive transactions. For example, a person may be able to deduce that two companies have exchanged contracts at a particular time. This could have commercial and market implications.

Storage of Information

Currently, the courts and legal practitioners store personal information relating to legal proceedings long after the matter has been completed using a number of different media including microfiche. Electronic storage increases the ease and reduces the expense of storing large amounts of information. A change from paper to electronic records requires a change in the security procedures and devices protecting stored information. As well, it is important to ensure that better storage mechanisms do not result in information being stored for longer than is actually required.

The Legal Framework

There are two main ways in which the law operates to ensure that information is used only for authorised purposes. The first is by imposing criminal or civil sanctions upon those who gain access to sensitive information without permission. The second is by requiring the party holding the information to ensure that it is handled in accordance with certain security and privacy standards.

Criminal and Civil Sanctions

To some extent, the deterrent effect of deeming any interceptive conduct to be a criminal offence helps to ensure the integrity of electronically communicated information. As noted earlier, such measures have been included in Victoria's proposed Electronic Commerce Framework Bill which, if enacted, amends the Crimes Act

1958 (Vic.) to include offences such as the gaining of access to data without authorisation, with an intent to defraud, or where the offender knew or ought to have known that the data was of a sensitive nature. These offences carry a maximum penalty of 10 years imprisonment. These provisions are in addition to existing legislative regulation of computer crimes at both federal and state level.

General law actions in trespass, breach of confidentiality, conversion, negligence and deceit may also be available against those who gain unauthorised access or cause damage to data, and provide remedies in the form of compensation for loss and damage and injunctions against further disclosure of information.

While this general legal framework is no doubt of assistance, its effectiveness in protecting the privacy of electronic information is limited. In practice, the nature of computer crimes gives rise to particular problems of enforcement.

Investigators face new challenges in establishing the identity of offenders, in the collection of sufficient evidence to result in a successful prosecution and in acting against offenders who are outside the legal jurisdiction.

Detailed inquiry into methods for improving effectiveness of prosecuting computer crimes is beyond the scope of this chapter. As any increase in the likelihood of detection for a breach of the law may have a deterrent effect upon potential offenders, work in this area is no doubt important in increasing the security of electronic technology. However, sanctions are largely reactive in nature and, therefore, are of themselves inadequate to fully address concerns regarding the prevention of a breach of privacy in relation to electronic information. Consequently, this section will focus upon the way in which the law is able to ensure that more proactive privacy measures are adopted in an effort to prevent any unauthorised access to data.

Standards of Privacy

There is no general right of individual privacy recognised at common law in Australia? Nonetheless, some protection of information is offered in particular areas by various privileges and duties. At both general law and under section 64(c) of the Legal Practice Act 1996 (Vic.), a legal practitioner has a duty to maintain the confidences of his or her clients. In particular, confidential information imparted in circumstances giving rise to an obligation of confidence may be legally protected.

This protection currently extends to most client information held by legal practitioners. Generally, information given to a court may be of a public nature. However, in certain cases the information will not be intended to be publicly disclosed.

More obvious examples include applications to the court by investigating officials to intercept the telecommunications of suspects, matters involving trade secrets and information given by complainants in sexual offence cases. Should this confidential information be electronically stored or transmitted by the court, then a duty would most likely be owed to ensure that reasonable precautions were taken to ensure no persons have unauthorised access. Where there is, or is likely to be, an unauthorised use of confidential information, the court may prevent disclosure by injunctive relief, the delivery up and destruction of the information, or the compensation for any loss suffered by the plaintiff arising as a result of the breach.

It remains open to question whether the interception of information communicated via email would be considered to be of a sufficiently confidential nature as to be protected by a duty of confidence. An analogy may be drawn with English and United States decisions where it has been held that parties communicating over the telephone accept the risk of their communication being intercepted. However, this approach has been criticised. The New Zealand Law Commission has concluded that such communications are of a confidential nature.

The American Bar Association's (ABA) Standing Committee on Ethics states that under most circumstances, a lawyer does not violate a client's confidentiality by transmitting documents via unencrypted electronic mail, 'because the mode of transmission affords a reasonable expectation of privacy from a technological and legal standpoint'. According to this opinion:

The same privacy accorded U.S. and commercial mail, land-line telephonic transmissions, and facsimiles applies to Internet e-mail. A lawyer should consult with the client and follow her instructions, however, as to the mode of transmitting highly sensitive information relating to the client's representation.

While mail can be lost or stolen and telephone conversations may be overheard by wiretap or eavesdropping, both provide reasonable expectations of privacy the ABA committee said. The ABA committee did not address the issue of the use of cellular or cordless phones.

Nonetheless, given the uncertainty of the law in this area, and the growing ease with which email communications can be intercepted, it is likely that some measures should be taken by the parties to the communication to prevent interception so as to ensure the communication remains confidential. Should legal practitioners or the courts fail to maintain the confidential nature of information they hold they may be in breach of a duty of confidence owed to the party providing the information.

The privacy of many communications between legal practitioners and clients, as well as documents relating to a proceeding, are protected by the doctrine of legal professional privilege. The privilege covers a narrower field of information than a duty of confidence. Generally, communications for both the sole purpose of legal advice and relating to a legal proceeding are protected from demands of disclosure.

Clearly, the loss of legal privilege would be of significant detriment to anyone appearing before a court. A case may be severely undermined if, for example, communications between the solicitor and client which reveal the weaknesses of the party's position could be accessed by the opposing side and tendered as evidence before the court. Increasing the likelihood that legal privilege may be lost could result in reluctance on the part of clients to be frank with their legal representatives and thereby affect access to and the effectiveness of the legal system.

Legal professional privilege only extends to the protection of confidential information. As discussed above in relation to confidentially, it is likely that communication of information via unprotected email, or otherwise unprotected information, would be inconsistent with any later claim that the information was of a confidential nature. While the law in the area is uncertain, clearly it would be prudent to ensure that legal practitioners adopt a reasonable standard of security and privacy so as to ensure the legal privilege of client information.

Legal practitioners, having a clear duty of care to act in the best interests of their client, may also be liable for damage resulting from any loss of privilege or confidentiality arising from their negligent conduct. It is even possible that a failure to implement reasonable security measures to protect the privacy of electronic communications may be held by the courts to constitute negligent conduct.

When assessing whether or not an allegation of negligence is made out, courts will take into account current industry practice. Clearly, increased use and availability of precautionary measures in relation to the handling of sensitive information would make it increasing difficult to sustain an argument that non-adoption of reasonable precautions was not in breach of a duty of care.

To some extent the privacy of individuals is protected by the Privacy Act 1988 (Cth). This Act imposes legal requirements concerning the handling of information. However, at present its application is limited to the regulation of the Commonwealth Government and its agencies, credit providers and handlers of tax file numbers.

Mandating Privacy Standards

A significant deficiency in the current privacy law framework is its general failure to regulate the conduct of those in the private sector that hold personal data. Moves to extend the law in this respect are fuelled by a growing concern in an apparent increase in the extent and sophistication of data warehousing and data mining technologies and data matching practices by some private companies.

A growing number of countries are adopting the 1980 OECD Privacy Guidelines in relation to data protection. These guidelines regulate the conduct of both the public and the private sector and prohibit the transfer of information to other countries where standards of privacy are inadequate.

In October 1998, at the OECD Ministerial level Conference held in Ottawa, Canada on 'A Borderless World: Realising the Potential of Global Electronic Commerce', OECD member countries (including Australia) issued a Ministerial Declaration on the Protection of Privacy on Global Networks.The Declaration reaffirms that:

> the technology-neutral principles of the 1980 OECD Privacy Guidelines continue to represent international consensus and guidance concerning the collection and handling of personal data in any medium, and provide a foundation for privacy protection on global networks.

The European Union also has been very active in the area of personal data protection. On 24 October 1995, the European Parliament and the Council adopted Directive 95/46/EC on the Protection of Individuals with Regard to the Processing of Personal Data and on the Free

Movement of Such Data. The Directive entered into effect on 25 October 1998. The Directive is intended:

(a) To establish a clear and stable regulatory framework to ensure:

  (i) a high level of protection for the privacy of individuals in all Member States; and

  (ii) the free movement of personal data within the European Union;

(b) to facilitate the development of electronic commerce by promoting consumer confidence and minimising differences between Member States' data protection rules; and

(c) to establish rules to ensure that personal data is only transferred to countries outside the EU when its continued protection is guaranteed.

While the EU Directive is principally intended to facilitate cross-border flows of personal data between all those involved in a private or public capacity in economic and social activity in the Member States, the Directive contains provisions relating to the transfer of personal data to 'third countries'—that is, non EU members. Article 25(1) provides:

> The Member States shall provide that the transfer to a third country of personal data which are undergoing processing or are intended for processing after transfer may take place only if, without prejudice to compliance with the national provisions adopted pursuant to the other provisions of this Directive, the third country in question ensures an adequate level of protection.

Other provisions of Article 25 give further definition to the concept of 'an adequate level of protection'.

It is essential, therefore, that Australia makes legislative provision for the protection of personal data if it is to take full advantage of the opportunities offered by the information economy. For example, with the increase in globalisation of legal practice, personal data may be transferred between teams of lawyers around the world working on the same project.

Australian Federal Privacy Commissioners National Principles: In February 1998, the Federal Privacy Commissioner released a recommended approach to the issue of information handling.The report outlines a set of National Principles for the Fair Handling of Personal Information (National Principles), which are in line with international standards and designed to assist the private sector in the development of their own voluntary privacy codes.

This is relevant in the context of article 26 of the EU Directive, which states that even if a 'third country' has inadequate national protection for personal information, such information may be exported on a 'case-by-case' basis if a particular organisation (such as a private company) can show that it specifically has adequate measures in place to protect the privacy of personal data. When issuing the National Principles, the Privacy Commissioner noted then that they would need to be reviewed within six to twelve months in the light of discussions on implementation, and in response to any issues that arise in practice. In particular it would be necessary to review the principles relating to law enforcement functions.

Those reviews were completed late in 1998, and a number of amendments were made. The law enforcement provisions were made more specific. A small number of changes were made to bring the principles more closely into line with the European Union's data protection framework. Other minor changes were introduced to clarify the meaning of particular provisions.

The federal Attorney General has observed that 'the National Principles have been drafted in such a way as to be capable of application in both the conventional and electronic environments.

Of particular relevance to the issue of the protection of information from unauthorised access is National Principle 4.1, which states:

> An organisation should take reasonable steps to protect the personal information it holds from misuse and loss and from unauthorised access, modification or disclosure.

Additionally, the storage of information is regulated by National Principle 4.2, which states:

> An organisation should take reasonable steps to destroy or permanently de-identify personal information if it is no longer needed for any purpose.

It is noted that a recent Senate Committee report has strongly criticised the National Principles as being 'a very weak and piecemeal approach to the issue of collection and protection of data'. However, it is also noted that when the Senate Committee made its findings, it did not have the benefit of seeing the revised version of the National Principle that was released in January 1999.

The Victorian Draft Data Protection Bill: In July 1998, the Victorian Government released a proposal for the development of a Data Protection Bill. A draft proposed bill was circulated for public comment in December 1998. The bill is based on the Commonwealth Privacy

Commissioner's National Principles and was facilitated by the work of the Victorian Data Protection Advisory Council.The aim of the proposed legislation is to provide a minimum standard in relation to the handling of personal information by both the public and private sector within Victoria. The regime would also facilitate the development of industry based voluntary codes which, once approved, would regulate the practice of the particular industry.

The Victorian Government has recently observed:

> Data protection primarily involves a careful balancing of two competing objectives: the first aims to inform and regulate the collection, use, storage, disclosure and quality of personal information; the second recognises that competing public interests, for example the free flow of information, may outweigh the individual's right to privacy. Without trust and confidence being established in the use of electronic services their potential use will remain just that—a potential use.

The Data Protection Bill (DPB) will protect the privacy of personal information handled by Victoria-based organisations and personal information handled in Victoria by business, State and local government and other organisations. It provides a 'light-handed legislative scheme', which aims to:

(a) implement the National Principles for the Fair Handling of Personal Information, so far as legally possible, to provide a uniform balance between the protection of information privacy and the free flow of information;

(b) provide equivalent standards for the handling of personal information by both the public and the private sectors; and

(c) ensure that commercial and other exchanges of information between Victoria and entities based overseas are not improperly impeded.

Part 1 of the bill contains general and definitional provisions and provides for certain exemptions from the bill's provisions, including:

(a) household or domestic collection of personal information;

(b) certain publicly available documents;

(c) the disclosure of personal information in certain circumstances by journalists;

(d) the use of non-identifying information by organisations compiling statistics or conducting other forms of research;

(e) documents subject to the Freedom of Information Act 1982 (Vic.); and

(f) other specific exemptions in relation to law enforcement agencies.

Part 1 also provides that any inconsistent provision in any other legislation will prevail, and refers to arrangements with the Commonwealth regarding the role of the federal Privacy Commissioner in the Victorian scheme.

Part 2 of the bill imposes obligations on companies and individuals to comply with the Information Privacy Principles (IPPs), which are set out in a schedule to the bill. These are based on the National Privacy Principles 'to the greatest extent possible, given legal and practical restrictions'.

IPPs will not apply retrospectively to the collection of information, but will regulate the use and disclosure of personal information, as well as prescribing rights to access information, regardless of when the information was collected. There is a phasing-in period of twelve months after the bill comes into force, which is expected some time after 1 January 2001.

It is noted that for the purposes of the bill, the status or effect of an act or practice is not affected by any outsourcing contract. This provision has been inserted because the Government:

> is committed to ensuring the information handling standards that apply to an organisation wishing to outsource its functions are the same standards that must be applied by the service provider.

Part 3 of the bill provides for the approval of codes of practice. An organisation may seek to discharge its duty to comply with an IPP by complying with an approved code of practice. This provides flexibility by allowing organisations to tailor their obligations to the specific needs of their business. Codes may create lesser or greater standards than those specified in IPPs, provided that they meet two criteria, to be assessed by the Victorian Privacy Commissioner:

(a) a code must substantially achieve the objectives of the bill; and

(b) a code must not be contrary to the public interest.

The Victorian Privacy Commissioner will be required to consult with the federal Privacy Commissioner in making a decision whether to approve a code.

Part 4 of the bill deals with the resolution of complaints by the Privacy Commissioner. In cases where a code of practice specifies a complaints mechanism, that mechanism must be followed first. Where complaints are not resolved satisfactorily at this stage, it is possible to refer the complaint to the Privacy Commissioner. The Privacy Commissioner is not established as a tribunal and cannot issue determinations that are binding on parties to a complaint. His or her main function is to conciliate complaints.

In the event that conciliation is unsuccessful, the Victorian Civil and Administrative Tribunal (VCAT) has a review function.VCAT also has a limited jurisdiction at first instance.VCAT may make binding determinations to resolve complaints. It can make orders including restraining or mandating conduct of the respondent, orders for compensation to a maximum of $100,000, orders for the correction of information or that certain other steps be taken.

Part 5 of the bill provides a mechanism for dealing with serious contraventions of approved codes of practice or the legislation by the issue of a compliance notice. The maximum penalty for failure to comply with a compliance notice is $60,000 for an individual and $300,000 for a corporation. The Privacy Commissioner's decision to issue a compliance notice is subject to review by VCAT.

Part 6 of the bill establishes the office of Privacy Commissioner, describes his or her functions and confers various powers. The functions of the Privacy Commissioner are very wide and include:

(a) promotion of IPPs;

(b) development of guidelines for compliance and model contractual terms;

(c) assessment of codes of conduct for compliance with information handling standards;

(d) conduct of investigations and conciliation of complaints;

(e) providing advice and training on the operation of the scheme;

(f) advising government on legislation and policies;

(g) monitoring developments in technology and data processing;

(h) undertaking educational programs about information privacy; and

(i) conducting and overseeing audits.

Part 7 of the bill contains miscellaneous provisions, while Part 8 deals with necessary amendments to Acts that interact with the data protection scheme. Despite its expressed intention to enact its own data protection legislation, the Victorian Government has recently said that it remains committed to the development of a suitable national privacy scheme:

> Clearly a national regime backed by federal legislation would be preferable. Should the Commonwealth's position on this issue change, and a suitable national regime for the private sector be developed, Victoria will vacate the field to the extent of the Commonwealth's powers.

Depending upon the speed and nature of developments at a national level, the Victorian Data Protection Bill is scheduled for introduction and passage through the State Parliament during 1999. Given the Victorian Government's preferred option, it is necessary therefore to consider developments in data protection at the Commonwealth level.

Recent Commonwealth Government Initiatives: The Privacy (Amendment) Bill 1998 (Cth) (the Outsourcing Bill) was passed by the House of Representatives on 1 April 1998, but was sent to the Senate Legal and Constitutional References Committee when it reached the Senate. Rather than simply consider the Privacy Amendment Bill, the Senate Committee decided to conduct a wide-ranging inquiry into privacy, including whether the private sector should be covered by national legislation. It tabled its final report in the Senate in March 1999. The bill lapsed when the Senate was prorogued for the October 1998 General Election and has not been restored to the notice paper. After examining the issue of privacy in the private sector, the Senate Committee concluded that:

> there is strong evidence of widespread community concern over the protection of privacy rights generally, fuelled by the rapid advances in technology, particularly in the areas of electronic commerce and the Internet.

Privacy protection currently provided by existing legislation and common law actions is inadequate and that, at this stage, 'private sector self-regulatory systems do not, of themselves, provide an adequate system of privacy protection in Australia'. The Senate Committee's main recommendation was that the Commonwealth Government:

> introduce legislation to provide privacy protection uniformly covering the public, private and the charitable and 'not for profit' sectors. The coverage of the bill should be as broad as possible and minimise the extent of exemptions.

The Senate Committee's preferred solution for addressing the need for privacy protection in the private sector is a co-regulatory model based on a model developed by the Commonwealth Attorney-General's Department. This comprises privacy protection based on flexible industry codes developed in cooperation with the Privacy Commissioner and backed by a legislative scheme.

The Commonwealth Government 'investigate mechanisms to achieve a cooperative legislative approach with the State and Territory Parliaments that could ensure effective legislation'.It urged the Government 'to move promptly' to develop a comprehensive national scheme for privacy protection, because 'an effective privacy protection regime is urgently required in Australia'. On 15 December 1998, the Commonwealth Attorney-General and the Minister for Communications, Information Technology and the Arts announced that the Federal Government would legislate to support and strengthen self-regulatory privacy protection in the private sector. A 'light touch legislative regime based on the Privacy Commissioner's National Principles for the Fair Handling of Personal Information' was proposed. It is intended that the scheme will be based on industry codes and apply a legislative framework only where industry codes are not adopted.

The scheme contains some exemptions. For example, businesses that hold no personal data other than employee records will not be affected by the legislation. Personal information collected and used by the media for journalistic purposes will also be exempt from the scheme. The federal Privacy Commissioner will assist business to implement the scheme.The Ministers opined that: 'This decision will provide a boost to electronic commerce by increasing the confidence of users that their personal data will be adequately protected'.

8

Consumers, Social Justice and World Market

The consumer movement enters this millennium with strengthened commitment to the fundamental principles that inspired us in the 20th century. Our movement is concerned not only with value for money for consumers but places the rights and choices of individual consumers in the context of social and economic justice for all.

Consumers International's Consumer Bill of Rights and the Consumers International-sponsored United Nations Guidelines for Consumer Protection reflect our view that consumer rights and protection can only be achieved as part of a global struggle for justice for all people.

In each era, the specific policies that advance our fundamental principles have evolved as economic, technological, political and social conditions have changed. This dynamic approach has enabled our movement to grow, maintain its relevance and be even more necessary in the new millennium.

We reaffirm our dedication to the goal of a just and equitable society for the world's six billion consumers. Many policies will help achieve such justice. At this World Congress, we have highlighted the following broad issues:

1. Global and national liberalised market economies will not by themselves eradicate poverty; indeed, they can worsen it and exacerbate inequalities. Positive social and economic measures are needed to eliminate poverty. Our movement, as part of civil society, should play a vigorous role in overcoming poverty and assuring that the poorest populations can at least meet their basic needs.

2. New scientific and technological developments have come at a rapid pace and will largely define the opportunities of the 21st century. Our movement must advocate policies that address these developments by embracing the opportunities they present and limiting their potential harmful effects to ensure that they have a positive effect on the health and well-being and quality of all our lives.

3. The globalised market economy has strengthened the power of global business interests and created global institutions with little or no accountability to community and general public interests. The consumer movement must work as part of a strong participative citizen movement that insists that the marketplace serves human rights and needs and that human interests are placed at the very core of business and governmental activity. Governance of both government and business activity must be improved.

4. Consumption and production patterns have an impact on the environment, and on the rights and needs of other people as consumers now and in the future. Our awareness of this should lead us to establish policies that help promote patterns of consumption and production that are sustainable and ethical.
5. Corrupt practices and poor standards of governance severely reduce the welfare of all consumers and compromise the attainment of their rights. Governments must commit themselves to effective measures to eradicate corruption and strengthen governance. The consumer movement must form alliances with national and international organisations of civil society dedicated to the control of corrupt practices and improvements in governance.

We are proud of the role consumer organisations all over the world have played in the struggle for a fair marketplace and social and economic justice for all. We are proud of the role Consumers International has played to help build and strengthen our movement and to bring our voices to regional and global forums. We are proud of our contribution to developing and promoting civil society values in a world that is increasingly inhospitable to those values.

Now in the 21st century, we rededicate ourselves to continuing to work for social and economic justice and to work with other public interest groups because we are all consumers and we are all citizens. The dramatic changes that have taken place over the last decades have created great challenges for us. They have also inspired us to develop the policies and strategies that can help bring social and economic justice to all the peoples of the world.

The essential starting point for Consumers International's policies is the eight basic rights of consumers. These are:

— the right to satisfaction of basic needs

— the right to safety

— the right to be informed

— the right to choose

— the right to be heard

— the right to redress

— the right to consumer education

— the right to a healthy environment

On the occasion of this, our first World Congress in Africa, we draw particular attention to the problems of establishing these rights in Africa and ensuring that the processes of globalisation contribute to social justice as well as economic development across the continent.

We call on international bodies and governments to establish and implement plans and programmes recognising the special needs of Africa. Measures should be taken to promote democracy and the respect of human rights, including economic, social, cultural, civil and political rights, to fight corruption, improve governance, reduce the burden of debt and promote a healthy and sustainable environment.

Consumer Policy

Consumer policy can contribute to poverty eradication, efficient markets, good governance and the promotion of human rights. All governments should actively pursue the three pillars of consumer policy – consumer legislation and regulations, consumer representation and the empowerment of individual consumers. The United Nation's Guidelines for Consumer Protection and Consumers International's Model Laws provide guidelines for some of the necessary elements of consumer policy.

All countries should have comprehensive consumer protection legislation, effectively implemented and including means to ensure access to justice. Specific measures are needed to protect consumers from hazardous products and technologies. Consumers International, working with its members, should encourage the introduction of appropriate legislation and governments should hold conferences on consumer protection in accordance with ECOSOC Resolution 1990/85.

Within this general framework, governments and international agencies should:

implement and adhere to the consumer policy recommendations contained in the UN Guidelines on Consumer Protection and such clauses included in other international and regional agreements;

- give special consideration to vulnerable and disadvantaged consumers;
- work to ensure requirements for and access for all to minimum consumption rights;
- facilitate public financing of consumer organisations where appropriate without compromising their independence;

— promote information strategies that support informed choices;

— provide the necessary safeguards, particularly for disadvantaged consumers, against inefficient, unfair and unjust markets;

— ensure the implementation and monitoring of international initiatives on chemicals in international trade (the UNEP Scheme and UN Guidelines), pesticides (FAO Code of Conduct) and breast milk substitutes (WHO Code);

— remove hazardous products from the market as soon as they are identified and ensure that product bans are applied equally to domestic consumption and to exports;

— take measures to prevent the export or transfer of high-risk technologies without proper consumer and environmental impact evaluation and safeguards, with penalties for those who break the rules, together with proper relief for injured parties;

— ensure that transparency and accountability prevail in the use of public resources;

— support and work jointly to promote access to justice nationally and internationally.

Consumers International and its members should place special emphasis on the needs and difficulties of vulnerable and disadvantaged consumers, especially where these are poorer consumers, women, children, older people, indigenous people and people with disabilities. Specific action includes:

— building distinct components into programmes;

— lobbying multilateral financial institutions and the UN to realign their policies and plans accordingly;

— seeking to ensure new technologies are of direct benefit to disadvantaged consumers;

— pressing for the adequate provision of appropriate goods and services for vulnerable groups and disadvantaged consumers, and their integration into all aspects of life.

Sustainable Consumption

Sustainable consumption, defined as reducing wasteful consumption and promoting more environmentally-sound products and services, has been recognised as a vitally important strategy in the effort to build a more sustainable world economy in the eight years since the adoption of Agenda 21.

Consumers International recognises that many of today's consumption patterns cannot be sustained without risk of exhausting the world's natural resources and of long-term and perhaps irreversible damage to the environment. Continued economic development is essential to meet human needs. However, strategies must be found to improve the quality of life for consumers while preserving the natural environment and ensuring equitable distribution of the world's resources.

Consumer organisations can play an important role in initiating and advocating change in consumption patterns, and have the means to provide consumers with information that allows them to make informed choices. They should also encourage governments and business to adopt policies and methods that will promote sustainable consumption, in accordance with the new sections of the UN Guidelines on Consumer Protection, adopted in 1999.

Business, governments and, where appropriate, international agencies should adopt plans of action to promote environmental protection and sustainable development, and specifically should:

— co-operate in the vital task of eradicating poverty as this is an indispensable requirement for establishing sustainable consumption;

— develop and apply technologies and methods that are environmentally sustainable for both poor and affluent consumers;

— work toward mandatory targets for major, sustainable reductions in greenhouse gas emissions;

— reduce wasteful energy production and consumption patterns and promote a supply of sustainable alternative energy sources;

— promote urban transport systems and policies, and forms of urban development, that minimise dependence on personal motor vehicles where they exacerbate pollution levels;

— review existing eco-labels and their demands critically, and reduce the number in use to a few which are internationally recognised and reliable;

— promote safe, efficient, ozone-protective and low-cost alternatives to CFCs, HFCs and HCFCs;

— promote biodiversity, natural ecosystems and water supplies, and promote sustainable agriculture and forestry practices and policies;

— promote investment in renewable resources and policies which influence demand.

Consumers International and its members are encouraged to build alliances with like-minded bodies and to lobby governments and international agencies to raise the level of public debate and awareness, to support policies and influence public opinion in order to:

— promote the steps above and others that reduce wasteful use of resources and prevent damage to the environment;

— reduce levels of resource use by developed countries, and by over-consuming sectors in developing countries;

— support environmental protection and standards while ensuring that these are not abused as trade barriers;

— ensure that animal protection measures are taken into account provided that these are not abused as trade barriers;

— ensure that consumers have sound information and education on the environmental impacts of their buying decisions and lifestyle choices;

— formulate a clear policy on the management of durability features in their testing and reporting activities, and live up to these policies in practice;

— generate public support for government policies described above;

— raise consumer awareness of production and marketing practices that promote expectations. and lifestyles not consistent with sound environmental policies.

Food Security and Food Safety

The world has enough food for its population, but over 800 million people suffer from hunger and food insecurity. For Consumers International, food security means that safe food is available, accessible and affordable by all people.

Food security is of concern to the consumer movement as all consumers have the right to sufficient and safe food. In protecting that right, governments and international agencies should:

- promote food security and improved access to food;
- give priority to the production of staple foods for domestic consumption, where necessary ensuring that agricultural policies are formulated to meet the needs of small-scale farmers (on whom most of developing countries households depend for their food needs and security) and low-income consumers;
- prohibit the use of patents on life forms which impede access for farmers and consumers and increase the dependency of developing economies;
- promote improved access to credit and technical assistance to the rural poor;
- support sound, transparent national land redistribution targeted at the most disadvantaged;
- seek to minimise waste in food production and distribution;
- support the development of national food control systems which are in line with international norms, in the interests of local consumers and to facilitate participation in international food markets;

— support sustainable agriculture practices and policies;

— ensure food is safe and truthfully represented;

— encourage and enable consumer participation in setting national and international food standards.

Consumers International and its members should promote sustainable local and regional food production and consumption patterns, for example by encouraging consumption of locally produced organic foods and foods in season.

Food safety is, above all, a public health issue. The precautionary principle should apply when scientific evidence is not conclusive enough to establish control measures based on a sound and accurate risk assessment but measures need to be taken for the purpose of protecting public health, public safety or the environment. Sound science is necessary for making safety decisions, but they must also take into account non-scientific factors such as economic concerns, ethical issues, environmental impact, and the benefits for the consumer to be obtained from the process or product.

Consumers International and its members recognise that the use of biotechnology and other new food technologies may provide important benefits. However, new technologies have raised many concerns for consumers about safety for human consumption, implications for the environment and potential social and economic impact. With this in mind, governments and international institutions should:

— require full pre-market evaluation and social and safety impact assessments of genetically modified (GM) foods and the products of other new food technologies to ensure that they are safe, environmentally sustainable and acceptable to consumers and impose a moratorium on the cultivation and marketing of new GM foods until this is done;

— desist from any attempts to intimidate other governments which restrict or prohibit such products based on their laws and evaluations of risks and benefits;

— prohibit the use of hormones and antibiotics as feed additives and veterinary drugs in the production of foodstuffs while their safety has not been proved; if any such use is permitted, to ensure that foods are clearly and explicitly labelled;

— promote active participation by consumer organisations in policy making, and ensure the transparency of decisions and the interests of those making the decisions;

— require clear and explicit labelling of irradiated foods, GM foods and other foods whose nature or methods of production raise, in the view of consumers, important concerns;

— promote methods for combating food-borne disease that are effective, safe, cost-effective, environmentally sustainable and acceptable to consumers.

Any food health claims should be clearly defined, easily understood, truthful and enforceable. Such claims should be strictly regulated at the national level and must be consistent with national health policy including nutrition policy and support such policies and goals. Health claims should be accompanied by specific consumer education.

The excessive and indiscriminate use of pesticides poses serious threats to health through direct contact in farming communities and through toxic residues in food. It may also undermine the development of sustainable agriculture. Governments and international agencies should promote pest control methods that minimise or eliminate pesticide use, in household and urban use as well as in food production, and encourage ecologically sound alternatives. National pesticide residue legislation should use health-based criteria.

Many pesticides are dangerous chemicals and regulation of their trade and use varies between countries. The requirement for prior informed consent from importing countries should be included in national legislation, international agreements and the FAO Code of Conduct on the distribution and use of pesticides.

Health

All consumers should have the means to meet their basic needs for a healthy life, and access to healthcare to help maintain it.

Consumers International and its members support the objectives and targets set out by the World Health Organisation (WHO) in its strategy document 'Health for All'. Effective primary health care should also be developed in accordance with the Alma Ata Declaration.

Action, which will contribute to these overall objectives, is also needed on specific health policies, including:

— the development of policies by national governments which guarantee universal access to health care for their citizens;

— the development by national governments of rational drug policies based on the WHO Essential Drug concept; all medicines should have significant therapeutic value, meet real medical need, be acceptably safe and provide satisfactory value for money. Programmes to provide consumers and prescribers with independent, scientifically sound drug information to stimulate rational drug use should accompany these policies. Consumer organisations should take part effectively in the definition, procedures and monitoring of national policies on drugs;

— the specification and promotion of patients' rights;

— the adoption and use within the WHO and among health regulators of Ethical Criteria for the Marketing of Drugs;

— support for campaigns to combat tobacco use and its promotion, and to develop and implement an evidence-based Framework Convention on Tobacco Control. Governments are urged to stop subsidising tobacco production and exports by promoting the production of alternative exports. Effective action to reduce tobacco use includes: banning advertising and sponsorship which uses products, brand names or logos; banning smoking in public places and workplaces; increased health education on the hazards of tobacco use; higher taxes and strong health warnings on tobacco products; and, corrective and counter advertising;

— full implementation of the WHO/UNICEF International Code of Marketing of Breast-milk Substitutes. Governments should condemn and restrict practices that promote inappropriate baby foods.

Consumers International and its members should establish strategic alliances with governments, health networks, research institutes, international organisations, media and others in order to develop programmes to work towards achieving these health objectives.

Trade and Economics

The daily lives of consumers across the world are directly affected by the actions of governments and international institutions in regulating and liberalising trade, investment and the practices of international business. Speculative financial flows, regional and multilateral trade liberalisation, and corporate mergers and acquisitions are of particular concern.

Consumers International and its members should seek to ensure that the interests and rights of consumers are recognised and protected in international trade and economic agreements.

Governments and international agencies should:

— ensure that trade and economic policies are formed with the involvement of, and take into account the interests of, all stakeholders, including consumers;

— ensure that all governments have the capacity to represent and negotiate on behalf of their people;

— cancel the debt of least developed countries;

— encourage the World Trade Organisation (WTO) and other such bodies to operate in an open and accessible manner and establish regular and effective consultation with consumer groups and other NGOs;

— reduce tariff and non-tariff trade barriers which have a negative impact on consumers and end 'voluntary' agreements which escape international trade rules;

— reform protectionist agricultural policies which produce expensive surpluses dumped on world markets;

— reassess the link between the Agreement on Trade Related Intellectual Property (TRIPs) and global agreements to protect biodiversity, recognising that consumers' rights come before those of business in the field of access to medicines, patenting life forms, biotechnology and biodiversity and that the rights of farmers in the developing world should be protected;

— through international co-operation, examine the effects of the global movement of capital on people and their nation states and seek to curb any negative effects of such movements which create further marginalisation and inequality;

— introduce legislation to set standards which transnational corporations (TNCs) must observe and agree a framework for monitoring TNC behaviour.

Business should:

— observe existing voluntary codes of conduct, such as the Organisation for Economic Co-operation and Development (OECD) Guidelines for Multinational Enterprises, the Code of Ethics on the International Trade in Chemicals, relevant articles of Agenda 21, and the UN Guidelines on Consumer Protection;

— engage with consumer organisations with a view to improving the transparency of business operations and understanding better local consumer needs.

Consumers International and its members should:

— research the impact of trade and economic liberalisation on the daily lives of consumers including environmental and social effects and inequality;

— work with international organisations as a way to influence and advise governments and others on consumer policies and priorities;

— promote the use of competition policy which enhances consumer welfare nationally;

— build the capacity of consumer organisations to influence national trade and competition policies.

Public Utilities

Changes in the management and regulation of public utilities — water, electricity, gas and telecommunications —and the technologies which they use, directly affect the price, quality and reliability of these services and access to them, and thus the most fundamental rights of consumers. The consumer interest should be the overriding concern in planning the future of these services, including decisions about their privatisation.

Essential requirements are: universal access, including if necessary special programmes to address the needs of poor consumers; accurate invoicing and forms of payment; formal published standards to ensure quality, durability and safety; the promotion of energy conservation; comprehensive and fair procedures for complaints and claims; and independent regulation supported by effective legal powers.

The first priority of all governments should be to make safe and affordable water available to all consumers.

Privatisation should not be regarded as necessary. In some circumstances, it may be appropriate, but this is unlikely to be the case where effective consumer protection legislation and institutions are not in place. Where privatisation is being considered, governments should ensure that the local community's views are properly considered to safeguard their interests, and that alternatives are thoroughly studied. Consumer organisations should have an active role in privatisation debates, which must be transparent and include public access to relevant documents.

Consumer Education

Consumer education is essential to provide the skills and knowledge to empower consumers and enable them to use their resources effectively and increase their awareness of their wider role in society.

Consumer education addresses not only problems of consumers individually but also of sustainable consumption, social justice, human rights, ethical values and poverty eradication. Consumer education contributes towards the formation of a participative, critical and competent citizenship.

All governments should be urged to incorporate consumer education as a mandatory part of the basic school curriculum. Consumers International and its members should promote the importance of consumer education programmes both to governments and to international agencies, and develop greater contacts with the media and use it for implementing programmes.

International co-operation provides a valuable means of increasing the expertise and information available to consumer organisations and educators. Consumers International and its members should continue to support consumer education networks and explore the possibility of creating and maintaining:

— a clearinghouse of consumer education material taking into account the importance of multilingual publications;

— a training centre based in a developing country for consumer activists and officials;

— a worldwide agreement with UNESCO and with institutions specialising in consumer education to promote it in as many countries as possible.

Business-sponsored teaching materials can undermine effective consumer education. A code of practice and/or guidelines for evaluating and countering this would be a valuable tool.

International Rules and Standards

International rules and standards have an important impact on the safe design, performance and fitness for purpose of products and services, and hence provide vital safeguards and protection for consumers. These rules and standards are made by a number of bodies.

Standards must be developed taking into account actual use by consumers, the range of consumers exposed to the product and different cultural and climatic needs of consumers in different regions.

Governments should only undertake harmonisation of standards where there is a clear benefit for consumers and where it is understood that the standards setting process must respect democratic values.

Consumers International and its members should play an active role in standardisation. They should participate in the development of Consumers International policies and in technical committees preparing national and international standards of consumer interest. They should act in co-operation with other international bodies representing consumers. All bodies responsible for standard setting should actively seek and facilitate the participation of consumer representatives in their work.

Consumers International and its members should:

— set up discussion networks on international standardisation;

— increase their work on the Codex Alimentarius, which has become a focus for setting global food standards following trade liberalisation and the establishment of the WTO;

— liaise closely with the International Organisation for Standardisation's consumer body (ISO/COPOLCO) and with other appropriate international and regional bodies, with the aim of achieving consumer representation on standards committees dealing with agreed priority issues for consumers;

— seek to ensure that all standards bodies operate in a transparent manner and develop standards by a clearly understood consensus process involving consumers.

Consumers International and its members encourage governments, the Codex Alimentarius Commission, FAO and WHO and other standards organisations, as appropriate, to:

— set up and/or support consumer participation in National Standards Bodies and their committees;

— assure adequate representation of the consumer interest and provide funds to enable consumer organisations to participate in appropriate standards work including relevant national, sub-regional and regional workshops, seminars and meetings;

— ensure democratic and transparent processes in standards making and the full participation of all countries;

— set up and/or support National Codex Committees with active consumer participation;

— increase public awareness and understanding of the Codex and standards process.

Product Testing

Product testing and research continues to be an essential part of the work of individual consumer organisations and of the consumer movement.

Consumers International should seek to stimulate research and testing activities in different regions through sharing experiences between testing organisations and newer groups, through training programmes and through structured regional testing programmes. There should be at least one organisation in each region that can act as a focus for co-ordinating testing expertise.

Information Technology and Media

The development of information technology and publishing and broadcast media provide many opportunities for empowering consumers and aiding the work of consumer organisations.

For these benefits to be exploited, both access and appropriate regulation need to be assured. Access needs particular attention to ensure that information technology does not promote the marginalisation of disadvantaged consumers and countries.

Consumers International and its members should seek to ensure that consumer interests are effectively represented at agencies dealing with international information technology and media policies - particularly in relation to issues of privacy, the regulation of advertising and services which cross national frontiers, and the regulation of interactive services. Changes in the media sector should also be monitored and policies sought which ensure diversity of ownership.

Effective consumer protection should be established for transactions made via the internet; these should be at least as effective and reliable as consumer protection for traditional transactions. Access, privacy, security, dispute resolution, and applicable laws and jurisdiction for the internet and electronic commerce should be included in any legal standard.

Where consumer rights depend on adherence to voluntary best practice guidelines, consumers need to be able to recognise internet shops and other services that offer high standards of consumer protection. The development of an internationally-recognised certification or labelling scheme should be supported.

An internationally-recognised third-party redress mechanism should be developed.

The feasibility of a worldwide computerised consumer database, information programmes which might be shared by consumer organisations, and an information technology guidance service for consumer organisation, should be assessed. These might cover information on dangerous products.

Children require special consideration with respect to advertising, recognising the principle, enshrined in the United Nations Convention on the Rights of the Child, that they should be free from exploitation 'prejudicial to any aspect of the child's welfare'.

Regulatory bodies, in consultation with consumer organisations, should introduce legislation which:

— provides special rules for advertising directed at children, or which is likely to be seen by children;

— covers advertising in all media and all advertising and marketing techniques and practices including children's clubs, television and radio, product packaging, direct mail, sponsorship and the internet.

Consumer Protection: Guidelines for Sustainable Consumption

Report of the UN Secretary-General

I. Background

1. The General Assembly adopted the guidelines for consumer protection in its resolution 39/248 of 9 April 1985. The guidelines constitute a comprehensive policy framework outlining what Governments can do to promote consumer protection in such areas as safety, economic interests of consumers, quality and distribution of goods and services, consumer education and information, and redress.

2. The guidelines provide an internationally recognized set of basic objectives, and were particularly designed for the Governments of developing and newly independent countries to use in structuring and strengthening consumer protection policies and legislation. The guidelines recognize that consumers often face imbalances in economic terms, education levels, and bargaining

power, and bear in mind that consumers should have the right of access to non-hazardous products, as well as the importance of promoting just, equitable and sustainable economic and social development.

3. More recently, there has been increasing concern with the linkages between consumption patterns and environmental protection, including discussions on the need to change consumption and production patterns to promote sustainable development.

   Agenda 21, adopted at the 1992 United Nations Conference on Environment and Development, includes a chapter entitled "Changing consumption patterns". As part of the implementation of Agenda 21, in 1995 the Commission on Sustainable Development established an international work programme on changing consumption and production patterns.

4. In 1995, the Commission on Sustainable Development also recommended that the guidelines for consumer protection be expanded to include guidelines on sustainable consumption patterns. 1/ In its resolution 1995/53, the Economic and Social Council requested the Secretary-General to elaborate guidelines in the area of sustainable consumption patterns.

5. In its resolution 1997/53, the Council welcomed the several initiatives of the United Nations, in partnership with international consumer organizations, donors and host Governments, in convening regional conferences on consumer protection to foster the implementation of the

guidelines and initiate the process of revising the guidelines and extending them into the area of sustainable consumption patterns and other possible areas.

6. The Council also requested the Secretary-General to continue work on the elaboration of the guidelines to cover sustainable consumption patterns through the convening of an interregional expert group meeting in collaboration with interested Governments, Consumers International and other concerned entities active in this field, taking into account the recommendations emanating from regional conferences on consumer protection. The Council recommended that the interregional expert group meeting elaborate specific recommendations for guidelines for sustainable consumption patterns for submission to the Council at its substantive session of 1998, through the Commission on Sustainable Development at its sixth session.

7. In response to the request of the Council, the Interregional Expert Group Meeting on Consumer Protection and Sustainable Consumption was convened at Sao Paulo, Brazil, from 28 to 30 January 1998. The meeting was organized by the Department of Economic and Social Affairs of the United Nations Secretariat, and was hosted by the environment secretariat of the state of S o Paulo and the Latin American Parliament. As requested by the Commission on Sustainable Development and the Economic and Social Council, Consumers International assisted in the substantive preparations for the meeting, taking into account the recommendations of regional conferences on consumer protection.

II. Development and implementation of the guidelines

8. In many countries, concern about consumer protection has grown in recent years, and Governments and consumer groups have become interested in the ideas and experiences of other countries. The guidelines for consumer protection, which are based on the experiences of many developed and developing countries, have assisted Governments in the identification of priorities.

   Economic growth in some countries, market liberalization in many countries, and democratic political reforms and the strengthening of civil society have all contributed to the interest in consumer protection. In response to requests from the Economic and Social Council, the Secetary-General has submitted two reports on progress achieved in the implementation of the guidelines since 1985.

9. The guidelines have responded to the growing international interest in consumer protection, and have contributed to that growth. In Africa, at the time of the adoption of the guidelines in 1985, six consumer organizations in four countries had been established; today, more than 40 African countries are host to more than 80 consumer organizations.

   Consumer rights are legally recognized in 13 Latin American and Caribbean nations, and in 7 of those countries they are also included in the Constitution. In Central America, four countries have created or strengthened legal norms in this area in recent years.

10. Although the majority of developed countries have institutional and regulatory frameworks in the field of consumer policy that generally cover the elements of the guidelines, the guidelines have been used as a reference for review and assessment of consumer protection policy in a number of those countries.

11. With increased recognition of the link between consumption patterns and environmental sustainability, a number of Governments and many consumer organizations have focused on ext ending consumer protection policies and programmes to cover environmental protection and other sustainable consumption issues.

12. The present report, which is based on the work of the Interregional Expert Group Meeting, has been prepared to assist the Commission on Sustainable Development and the Economic and Social Council in their consideration of the expansion of the guidelines for consumer protection to include guidelines for sustainable consumption patterns.

13. The report of the Co-Chairmen on the Interregional Expert Group Meeting is contained in the annex to the present report; it includes proposed new elements on sustainable consumption for addition to the guidelines for consumer protection.

I. Organization of the Meeting

1. In accordance with Economic and Social Council resolution 1997/53, the Department of Economic and Social Affairs of the United Nations Secretariat, in cooperation with the environment secretariat of

the state government of S o Paulo, convened the Interregional Expert Group Meeting on Consumer Protection and Sustainable Consumption at Sao Paulo, Brazil, from 28 to 30 January 1998. Approximately 50 people participated, including representatives of Governments, consumer organizations, business and industry, academics, non-governmental organizations and international organizations.

2. The Meeting was chaired by Ambassador Celso Amorim, Permanent Representative of Brazil to the United Nations, and Mr. Fabio Feldman, Secretary of the environment secretariat of the state government of Sao Paulo.

3. The work of the Meeting, which was conducted in plenary and working group sessions, focused on a background paper prepared for the meeting by the Division for Sustainable Development of the United Nations Secretariat, including proposed new guidelines prepared by Consumers International on the basis of extensive regional consultations. During the Meeting, additional proposals were presented and considered.

4. The Meeting did not attempt to reach consensus on precise wording for new guidelines but focused on identifying the issues relating to sustainable consumption that should be incorporated into consumer protection policy and making recommendations on how they might be effectively addressed.

5. The Meeting focused on issues related to sustainable consumption. It did not review or revise the existing text of the guidelines or consider

other areas in which the guidelines might be extended. In some cases, however, it appeared that sustainable consumption could best be integrated into the guidelines by introducing additional words into existing paragraphs, without otherwise changing the existing text.

6. The present report is a summary by the Co-Chairmen of the work of the Meeting; it contains the general conclusions of the Meeting and proposed new elements on sustainable consumption for addition to the guidelines for consumer protection.

II. General conclusions of the Meeting

7. Sustainable consumption is an essential part of sustainable development and is losely tied to sustainable production. Sustainable production concerns the supply side, focusing on the economic, social and environmental impact of production processes, while sustainable consumption addresses the demand side, focusing on consumers' choices of goods and services, such as food, shelter, clothing, mobility and leisure, to fulfil basic needs and improve the quality of life.

8. Measures to promote sustainable consumption affect not only the products and services directly used by consumers, but also the energy and materials consumed in production processes and the wastes generated throughout the product life cycle, from raw material extraction through disposal or reuse.

9. In promoting sustainable consumption, Governments should act in partnership with all members of society. Particular attention should be paid to the significant role played by women and households as consumers. Governments should actively support consumer organizations and other organizations of civil society in promoting sustainable consumption.

10. To achieve more sustainable consumption, it is crucial to promote public participation in policy-making for the management and use of natural resources that are essential for meeting basic human needs, in particular freshwater, land and ocean resources.

11. Sustainable consumption requires that consumers, communities, businesses and organizations of civil society be aware of the potential environmental effects of products and services, including local and global impacts. Information, infrastructure and facilities should be available to consumers wishing to change their consumption patterns.

12. Consumer empowerment for sustainable consumption requires both informed choice and preventive and remedial mechanisms in cases of wrongdoing.

13. As indicated in paragraph 8 of the guidelines, in applying any procedures or regulations for consumer protection, including sustainable consumption, due regard should be given to ensuring that they do not become barriers to international trade and that they are consistent with international trade obligations.

14. Recognizing that the major cause of the continued deterioration of the global environment is the unsustainable pattern of consumption and production, particularly in industrialized countries, Governments should cooperate in changing consumption patterns at the global level. In so doing, they should be guided by the principle of common but differentiated responsibilities and the equitable sharing among the world population of environmental resources and the environment's capacity to absorb waste.

15. Developed countries should support developing countries in promoting sustainable development and consumption, in particular through financial assistance, transfer of environmentally sound technologies, support for indigenous research and development capabilities, and better access to markets.

16. Governments should fulfil their obligations under international environmental agreements, including the Montreal Protocol on Substances that Deplete the Ozone Layer, the United Nations Framework Convention on Climate Change, the Convention on Biological Diversity and Agenda 21.

17. A review and revision mechanism for these guidelines should be established nder the aegis of the United Nations so as to assess progress in their implementation by Member States and to revise them as necessary. The Secretary-General should report regularly on the status of their implementation. Technical assistance should be made available to countries that may encounter difficulties in collecting and processing the required data.

I. Objectives

1. Taking into account the interests and needs of consumers in all countries, particularly those in developing countries; recognizing that consumers often face imbalances in economic terms, educational levels, and bargaining power; and bearing in mind that consumers should have the right of access to non-hazardous products, as well as the right to promote just, equitable and sustainable economic and social development (open bold) and environmental protection, (close bold)these guidelines for consumer protection have the following objectives:

   (a) To assist countries in achieving or maintaining adequate protection for their population as consumers;

   (b) To facilitate production and distribution patterns responsive to the needs and desires of consumers;

   (c) To encourage high levels of ethical conduct for those engaged in the production and distribution of goods and services to consumers;

   (d) To assist countries in curbing abusive business practices by all enterprises at the national and international levels which adversely affect consumers;

   (e) To facilitate the development of independent consumer groups;

   (f) To further international cooperation in the field of consumer protection;

(g) To encourage the development of market conditions which provide consumers with greater choice at lower prices.

II. General principles

2. Governments should develop, strengthen or maintain a strong consumer protection policy, taking into account the guidelines set out below and international agreements, such as those related to sustainable development. In so doing, each Government should set its own priorities (open bold) and time-bound targets for the protection of consumers in accordance with the economic, social and environmental (close bold) circumstances of the country and the needs of its population, bearing in mind the costs and benefits of proposed measures.

3. The legitimate needs which the guidelines are intended to meet are the following:

   (a) The protection of consumers from hazards to their health and safety;

   (b) The promotion and protection of the economic interests of consumers;

   c) Access of consumers to adequate information to enable them to make informed choices according to individual wishes and needs;

   (d) Consumer education;

   (e) Availability of effective consumer redress;

   (f) Freedom to form consumer and other relevant groups or organizations and the opportunity of such organizations to present their views in decision-making processes affecting them;

(g) The promotion of sustainable consumption patterns.

4. Governments should provide or maintain adequate infrastructure to develop, implement and monitor consumer protection policies. Special care should be taken to ensure that measures for consumer protection are implemented for the benefit of all sectors of the population, particularly the rural population.

5. All enterprises should obey the relevant laws and regulations of the countries in which they do business. They should also conform to the appropriate provisions of international standards for consumer protection to which the competent authorities of the country in question have agreed.

6. The potential positive role of universities and public and private enterprises in research should be considered when developing consumer protection policies.

III. Guidelines

7. The following guidelines should apply both to home-produced goods and services and to imports.

8. In applying any procedures or regulations for consumer protection, due regard should be given to ensuring that they do not become barriers to international trade and that they are consistent with international trade obligations.

A. Physical safety

9. Governments should adopt or encourage the adoption of appropriate measures, including legal

systems, safety regulations, national or international standards, voluntary standards and the maintenance of safety records to ensure that products are safe for either intended or normally foreseeable use.

10. Appropriate policies should ensure that goods produced by manufacturers are safe for either intended or normally foreseeable use. Those responsible for bringing goods to the market, in particular suppliers, exporters, importers, retailers and the like (hereinafter referred to as "distributors"), should ensure that while in their care these goods are not rendered unsafe through improper handling or storage and that while in their care they do not become hazardous through improper handling or storage. Consumers should be instructed in the proper use of goods and should be informed of the risks involved in intended or normally foreseeable use. Vital safety information should be conveyed to consumers by internationally understandable symbols wherever possible.

11. Appropriate policies should ensure that if manufacturers or distributors become aware of unforeseen hazards after products are placed on the market, they should notify the relevant authorities and, as appropriate, the public without delay. Governments should also consider ways of ensuring that consumers are properly informed of such hazards.

12. Governments should, where appropriate, adopt policies under which, if a product is found to be seriously defective and/or to constitute a

substantial and severe hazard even when properly used, manufacturers and/or distributors should recall it and replace or modify it, or substitute another product for it; if it is not possible to do this within a reasonable period of time, the consumer should be adequately compensated.

B. Promotion and protection of consumers' economic interests

13. Government policies should seek to enable consumers to obtain optimum benefit from their economic resources. They should also seek to achieve the goals of satisfactory production and performance standards, adequate distribution methods, fair business practices, informative marketing and effective protection against practices which could adversely affect the economic interests of consumers and the exercise of choice in the market-place.

14. Governments should intensify their efforts to prevent practices which are damaging to the economic interests of consumers through ensuring that manufacturers, distributors and others involved in the provision of goods and services adhere to established laws and mandatory standards. Consumer organizations should be encouraged to monitor adverse practices, such as the adulteration of foods, false or misleading claims in marketing and service frauds.

15. Governments should develop, strengthen or maintain, as the case may be, measures relating to the control of restrictive and other abusive business

practices which may be harmful to consumers, including means for the enforcement of such measures. In this connection, Governments should be guided by their commitment to the Set of Multilaterally Agreed Equitable Principles and Rules for the Control of Restrictive Business Practices adopted by the General Assembly in resolution 35/63 of 5 December 1980.

16. Governments should adopt or maintain policies that make clear the responsibility of the producer to ensure that goods meet reasonable demands of durability, utility and reliability, and are suited to the purpose for which they are intended, and that the seller should see that these requirements are met. Similar policies should apply to the provision of services.

17. Governments should encourage fair and effective competition in order to provide consumers with the greatest range of choice among products and services at the lowest cost.

18. Governments should, where appropriate, see to it that manufacturers and/or retailers ensure adequate availability of reliable after-sales service and spare parts.

19. Consumers should be protected from such contractual abuses as one-sided standard contracts, exclusion of essential rights in contracts, and unconscionable conditions of credit by sellers.

20. Promotional marketing and sales practices should be guided by the principle of fair treatment of consumers and should meet legal requirements. This requires the provision of the information

necessary to enable consumers to take informed and independent decisions, as well as measures to ensure that the information provided is accurate.

21. Governments should encourage all concerned to participate in the free flow of accurate information on all aspects of consumer products.

21a. Governments should promote consumer access to non-misleading information about the environmental impact of products and services through such means as eco-labelling schemes, product information hotlines, product profiles, environmental reports by industry, and information centres for consumers. They should also promote internationally recognized symbols for environmental labelling.

21b. Governments should take measures against misleading environmental claims or information in advertising and other marketing activities. The development of advertising codes and standards for the regulation and verification of environmental claims, backed by legal sanctions, should be promoted.

22. Governments should, within their own national context, encourage the formulation and implementation by business, in cooperation with consumer organizations, of codes of marketing and other business practices to ensure adequate consumer protection. Voluntary agreements may also be established jointly by business, consumer organizations and other interested parties. These codes should receive adequate publicity.

23. Governments should regularly review legislation pertaining to weights and measures and assess the adequacy of the machinery for its enforcement.

C. Standards for the safety and quality of consumer goods and services

24. Governments should, as appropriate, formulate or promote the elaboration and implementation of standards, voluntary and other, at the national and international levels for the safety and quality of goods and services and give them appropriate publicity. National standards and regulations for product safety and quality should be reviewed from time to time, in order to ensure that they conform, where possible, to generally accepted international standards.

25. Where a standard lower than the generally accepted international standard is being applied because of local economic conditions, every effort should be made to raise that standard as soon as possible.

26. Governments should encourage and ensure the availability of facilities to test and certify the safety, quality and performance of essential consumer goods and services.

D. Distribution facilities for essential consumer goods and services

27. Governments should, where appropriate, consider:

    (a) Adopting or maintaining policies to ensure the efficient distribution of goods and services to consumers; where appropriate, specific policies should be considered to ensure the distribution of essential goods and services where this distribution is endangered, as could be the case particularly in rural areas. Such policies could include assistance for the creation of adequate storage and retail facilities in rural centres, incentives for consumer self-help and better control of the conditions under which essential goods and services are provided in rural areas;

(b) Encouraging the establishment of consumer cooperatives and related trading activities, as well as information about them, especially in rural areas.

27a. Governments should develop policies, including pricing policies, for public and private utilities to ensure the highest efficiency of service delivery and resource conservation.

E. Measures enabling consumers to obtain redress

28. Governments should establish or maintain legal and/or administrative measures to enable consumers or, as appropriate, relevant organizations to obtain redress through formal or informal procedures that are expeditious, fair, inexpensive and accessible. Such procedures should take particular account of the needs of low-income consumers.

29. Governments should encourage all enterprises to resolve consumer disputes in a fair, expeditious and informal manner, and to establish voluntary mechanisms, including advisory services and informal complaints procedures, which can provide assistance to consumers.

30. Information on available redress and other dispute-resolving procedures should be made available to consumers.

F. Education and information programmes

31. Governments should develop or encourage the development of general consumer education and information programmes, including information on the environmental impacts of consumption patterns and the benefits of changes in consumption, bearing in mind the cultural traditions of the people concerned. The aim of such programmes should be to enable people to act as discriminating consumers, capable of making an informed choice of goods and services, and conscious of their rights and responsibilities. In developing such programmes, special attention should be given to the needs of disadvantaged consumers, in both rural and urban areas, including low-income consumers and those with low or non-existent literacy levels. Consumer groups and other organizations of civil society should be involved in these educational efforts, and programmes in developing countries should be supported by international agencies.

32. Consumer education should, where appropriate, become an integral part of the basic curriculum of the educational system, preferably as a component of existing subjects.

33. Consumer education and information programmes should cover such important aspects of consumer protection as the following:

    (a) Health, nutrition, prevention of food-borne diseases and food adulteration;

    (b) Product hazards;

(c) Product labelling;

(d) Relevant legislation, how to obtain redress, and agencies and organizations for consumer protection;

(e) Information on weights and measures, prices, quality, credit conditions and availability of basic necessities;

(f) Pollution and environment;

(g) Efficient use of materials, energy and water;

(h) Advertising and marketing.

34. Governments should encourage consumer organizations and other interested groups, including the media, to undertake education and information programmes, particularly for the benefit of low-income consumer groups in rural and urban areas.

35. Business should, where appropriate, undertake or participate in factual and relevant consumer education and information programmes.

36. Bearing in mind the need to reach rural consumers and illiterate consumers, Governments should, as appropriate, develop or encourage the development of consumer information programmes in the mass media.

37. Governments should organize or encourage training programmes for educators, mass media professionals and consumer advisers, to enable them to participate in carrying out consumer information and education programmes.

FF. Promotion of sustainable consumption

FF1. Sustainable consumption means meeting the needs of present and future generations for goods and services in ways that are economically, socially and environmentally sustainable. Since sustainable consumption depends on the availability of environmentally sound goods and services, it is closely tied to sustainable production.

FF2. Responsibility for sustainable consumption is shared by all members and organizations of society, with Government, business, labour organizations, and consumer and environmental organizations playing particularly important roles. Governments have the ultimate responsibility for developing and implementing policies for sustainable consumption and for integrating those policies with other public policies. Government policy-making should be conducted in consultation with business, consumer and environmental organizations, and other concerned groups. Business has a particular responsibility for promoting sustainable consumption through the design, production and distribution of goods and services, as well as a responsibility for their recycling and disposal. Consumer and environmental organizations have a responsibility for promoting public participation and debate on sustainable consumption, for informing consumers, and for working with Government and business towards sustainable consumption.

FF3. Governments, in partnership with business and organizations of civil society, should develop and implement policies that promote sustainable consumption through a mix of policies that could include regulations; economic and social instruments; sectoral policies, such as policies on land use, transport and housing; and the removal of subsidies that promote unsustainable patterns of consumption and production.

FF4. Sustainable consumption policies should promote the eradication of poverty, the satisfaction of the basic human needs of all members of society, and the reduction of inequality within and between countries.

FF5. With due regard to the principle of common but differentiated responsibilities, Governments should promote the design, development and use of products and services that are energy and resource efficient, non-toxic and safe, taking into account their full life cycle, including raw material extraction, production, distribution, use and disposal. Strategies for product improvement include extending product life and facilitating product repair, reuse and recycling.

FF6. Governments should promote innovative efforts by small and medium-sized enterprises to develop and market innovative products and services that promote sustainable consumption. Exports of sustainably produced products from developing countries should be promoted.

FF7. Governments should promote conservation of energy and the transition to renewable energy sources.

FF8. Governments should promote the development and use of national and international environmental standards for products and services, including production processes, with due regard to their impact on market access and competitiveness. Such standards should not result in unjustified restrictions on trade.

FF9. Governments should encourage, develop and support independent environmental testing of products, as well as international cooperation on joint testing, the development of common testing procedures and training.

FF10. Governments should ban or severely restrict environmentally harmful use of substances, such as those listed in the Basel Convention on the Control of Transboundary Movements of Hazardous Wastes and Their Disposal. New potentially hazardous substances should be tested for their long-term environmental impact prior to distribution. At the same time, Governments should encourage the development of environmentally sound alternatives for such materials, while promoting the use of the least damaging products and processes in the short term. The development of such alternatives can be encouraged through financial and other incentives, and through international cooperation in the development and transfer of clean technologies.

FF11. Governments should promote awareness of the health-related benefits of sustainable consumption and production patterns, taking into account both direct effects on individual health and collective effects through environmental protection.

FF12. Governments, in partnership with other organizations, should encourage the transformation of unsustainable consumption patterns through the development and use of services and new technologies that can meet consumer needs while reducing pollution and depletion of natural resources, including information and communication technologies.

FF13. Governments are encouraged to create or strengthen effective regulatory agencies addressing various aspects of sustainable consumption. They should periodically review the mandate and effectiveness of those agencies to ensure best practices in consumer protection, environmental assessment and law enforcement. Government agencies concerned with different aspects of sustainable consumption should cooperate and exchange experiences to maximize their effectiveness, and should work in cooperation with consumer organizations.

FF14. Governments should consider measures to promote pricing of products and services that takes account of environmental costs and promotes sustainable consumption. Governments should promote comprehensive analysis of all environmental costs and benefits, the internalization of environmental costs and the use of economic instruments, taking into account such principles as the "polluter pays" principle and full cost for resources (also known as the "user pays" principle). Governments should consider differentiated pricing as a way to ensure that disadvantaged people can fulfil their basic needs

FF15. Governments should make use of a range of economic instruments for promoting sustainable consumption. Taxation systems should be designed and implemented to provide disincentives for unsustainable practices and incentives for more sustainable practices.

FF16. Governments should implement natural resource accounting to reflect the impact of consumption and production patterns and policies on the environment, and should provide information to consumers on the impact of their consumption patterns. Governments, in cooperation with business and other groups, should develop comparable indicators, methodologies and databases for measuring progress towards sustainable consumption at all levels, including households. This information should be made publicly available.

FF17. Governments should promote sustainable transportation, including through policies to reduce the use of cars in urban centres, reduce unnecessary movement of goods, promote efficient public transportation systems, and promote more energy-efficient and less polluting vehicles. Governments should develop and implement standards for air quality, and should cooperate with the automobile industry in the development and implementation of standards for motor vehicle emissions and fuel economy.

FF18. Governments should develop urban planning and construction policy to ensure sustainable shelter and infrastructure for all, with particular attention to the needs of disadvantaged people. Within the construction sector, Governments should promote the use of environmentally sound building materials and the conservation of land and energy by appropriate design.

FF19. Governments and international agencies should take the lead in introducing sustainable practices in their own operations, in particular through their procurement policies. Government procurement should encourage the development and use of environmentally sound products and services.

FF20. Governments and international organizations should undertake and promote research on consumer behaviour and related environmental damage in order to identify ways to make consumption patterns more sustainable while meeting the basic human needs of all people.

G. Measures relating to specific areas

38. In advancing consumer interests, particularly in developing countries, governments should, where appropriate, give priority to areas of essential concern for the health of the consumer, such as food, water and pharmaceuticals. Policies should be adopted or maintained for product quality control, adequate and secure distribution facilities, standardized international labelling and information, as well as education and research programmes in these areas. Government guidelines in regard to specific areas should be developed in the context of the provisions of this document.

39. Food. When formulating national policies and plans with regard to food, Governments should take into account the need of all consumers for food security

and should support and, as far as possible, adopt standards from the Food and Agriculture Organization of the United Nations and the World Health Organization Codex Alimentarius or, in their absence, other generally accepted international food standards. Governments should maintain, develop or improve food safety measures, including, inter alia, safety criteria, food standards and dietary requirements and effective monitoring, inspection and evaluation mechanisms.

39a. Governments should promote sustainable agricultural policies and practices, the conservation of biodiversity, and the protection of soil and water through nutrient recycling, recognizing traditional knowledge. Governments should move towards eliminating subsidies and other incentives for unsustainable agricultural practices.

39b. Governments should introduce controls on genetically engineered foods and crop varieties, based on long-term risk assessment, to ensure that they are safe for people and the environment and are compatible with sustainable agriculture. Government controls should encompass both the production process and the final product in an open and transparent fashion, and should ensure that products are labelled taking consumer concerns into account.

40. Water. Governments should, within the goals and targets set for the International Drinking Water Supply and Sanitation Decade, formulate, maintain or strengthen national policies to improve the supply, distribution and quality of water for drinking.

Due regard should be paid to the choice of appropriate levels of service, quality and technology, the need for education programmes and the importance of community participation.

41. Pharmaceuticals. Governments should develop or maintain adequate standards, provisions and appropriate regulatory systems for ensuring the quality and appropriate use of pharmaceuticals through integrated national drug policies which could address, inter alia, procurement, distribution, production, licensing arrangements, registration systems and the availability of reliable information on pharmaceuticals.

In so doing, Governments should take special account of the work and recommendations of the World Health Organization on pharmaceuticals.

For relevant products, the use of that organization's Certification Scheme on the Quality of Pharmaceutical Products Moving in International Commerce and other international information systems on pharmaceuticals should be encouraged. Measures should also be taken, as appropriate, to promote the use of international non-proprietary names (INNs) for drugs, drawing on the work done by the World Health Organization.

42. In addition to the priority areas indicated above, Governments should adopt appropriate measures in other areas, such as pesticides and chemicals in regard, where relevant, to their use, production and storage, taking into account such relevant health and environmental information as Governments may require producers to provide and include in the labelling of products.

IV. International cooperation

43. Governments should, especially in a regional or subregional context:

   (a) Develop, review, maintain or strengthen, as appropriate, mechanisms for the exchange of information on national policies and measures in the field of consumer protection;

   (b) Cooperate or encourage cooperation in the implementation of consumer protection policies to achieve greater results within existing resources. Examples of such cooperation could be collaboration in the setting up or joint use of testing facilities, common testing procedures, exchange of consumer information and education programmes, joint training programmes and joint elaboration of regulations;

   (c) Cooperate to improve the conditions under which essential goods are offered to consumers, giving due regard to both price and quality. Such cooperation could include joint procurement of essential goods, exchange of information on different procurement possibilities and agreements on regional product specifications.

44. Governments should develop or strengthen information links regarding products which have been banned, withdrawn or severely restricted in order to enable other importing countries to protect themselves adequately against the harmful effects of such products.

45. Governments should work to ensure that the quality of products, and information relating to

such products, does not vary from country to country in a way that would have detrimental effects on consumers.

45a. Developed country Governments, in cooperation with business and international organizations, should promote and finance the transfer of environmentally sound technologies and related know-how to developing countries to enable them to meet the needs of consumers in a sustainable manner.

45b. Governments in developing countries, with support from developed countries and international organizations, should cooperate in South-South transfer of environmentally sound technologies and know-how. Governments and international organizations should also identify and develop opportunities for the transfer of environmentally sound technologies and practices developed in developing countries to developed countries, with adequate remuneration.

45c. Governments and business should work together to devise new and innovative mechanisms for financing the transfer of environmentally sound technologies, such as by creating an international fund. Developing countries should also be able to use compulsory licensing systems to gain access to environmentally sound technologies, in a manner consistent with international agreements on intellectual property rights.

46. Governments should work to ensure that policies and measures for consumer protection are implemented with due regard to their not becoming barriers to international trade, and that they are consistent with international trade obligations.

Bibliography

C.M. Bowman, P.B. Danzig, U. Manber, M. Schwartz, "Scalable Internet Resource Discovery: Reserach Problems and Approaches," Communications of the ACM, August 1994.

Ed Krol, The Whole Internet User's Guide and Catalog, (Sebastopol, CA: O'Reilly & Assoc., 1992).

"Electronic Billboards on the Digital Superhighway, a Report of the Working Group on Internet Advertising", The Coalition for Networked Information, March 18, 1994.

"Home Shopping Network—Company Report", Hanifen, Imhoff Inc., July 20, 1994.

Hinden, M. "IP Next Generation Overview", Internet Draft, October 1994.

"Information Superhighway: Issues Affecting Development" (GAO/RECD-94-22285), September 30, 1994.

"Interactive Advertising in an Online World", Information Week, October 3, 1994.

J.S. Rosenberg, "Copyright of Way on the Information Highway", Searcher, March 1994, p. 36

Johnson, David B., Andrew Myles, and Charles Perkins, "The Internet Mobile Host Protocol (IMHP)", Internet Draft, February 14, 1994.

Kim, B.G. and Wang P., "ATM Network: Goals and Challenges", Communications of the ACM, February 1995.

Medvinsky Gennady and B. Clifford Neuman, "NetCash: A Design for Practical Electronic Currency on the Internet",

Proceedings of the first ACM conference on Computer and Communication Security, November 1993.

Perkins Charles E. and Pravin Bhagwat, "A Mobile Networking System Based on Internet Protocol", IEEE Personal Communications, First quarter, 1994.

Request for Comments: 1192, "Commercialisation of the Internet", B. Kahin, Ed., November 1990, Harvard University.

Richard Chang, "Business Promote Smart Card as Computer in Wallet", The Reuter European Business Report, September 14, 1994.

"The Future of Electronic Commerce Explored at EM 2000", SIMBA Information Inc's Electronic Marketplace 2000 trade show, Electronic Marketplace Reports, March 15, 1994.

Vetter Ronald J., "ATM Concepts, Architectures, and Protocols", Communications of the ACM, February 1995.

Index